Leadership
Strategies
for
Community College
Executives

Gunder Myran
George A. Baker III
Beverly Simone
Tony Zeiss

Community College Press®
A division of the American Association of Community Colleges
Washington, D.C.

The American Association of Community Colleges (AACC) is the primary advocacy organization for the nation's community colleges. The association represents 1,100 two-year, associate degree–granting institutions and more than 10 million students. AACC promotes community colleges through six strategic action areas: national and international recognition and advocacy, learning and accountability, leadership development, economic and workforce development, connectedness across AACC membership, and international and intercultural education. Information about AACC and community colleges may be found at www.aacc.nche.edu.

Design: Brian Gallagher Design
Editor: Deanna D'Errico
Printer: Graphic Communications, Inc.

Community College Press
American Association of Community Colleges
One Dupont Circle, NW
Suite 410
Washington, DC 20036

Printed in the United States of America.

ISBN 0-87117-347-6

Contents

Figures and Tables

Preface

This book is about applied leadership. It is about what community college presidents and executive team members actually *do* to carry out their leadership responsibilities daily. The book is intended as a handbook on leadership practices for use by community college presidents, executive teams, governing boards, administrators, and faculty leaders, as well as graduate students interested in careers in community college leadership. This book will be helpful to community college leaders at any stage of their careers, but it is intended especially for new presidents and executives.

We have organized this book to address several areas of strategy that we have found to be in use by community college leaders around the country. Each of these strategic areas is discussed in a separate chapter, but in the day-to-day reality of leading a college, they are and should be overlapping and integrated. If this book has one central message, it is that an effective strategy is not a one-time event, but an ongoing series of actions, decisions, and relationships that move an institution toward fulfillment of its mission, vision, and core strategies.

Part I, "A Framework for Leadership Strategies," contains three chapters. Chapter 1, an overview of leadership strategies, provides a framework for the rest of the book. It presents the foundational statements, strategic framework, and execution strategies discussed in the remaining chapters. It also offers a perspective on how to lead the community college to the highest level of transformational change. Chapter 2, on achieving transformational change, provides a conceptual foundation for the strategic framework outlined in chapter 1. Chapter 3 addresses strategies for designing the organization to achieve its mission, vision, and core strategies.

Chapters 4–9 are the heart of the book. In these chapters we examine ways in which effective community college leaders make operational the principles of the strategic framework. In doing so, we address in turn the execution strategies in major areas of community college operations. Part II, "Execution Strategies," focuses on policy development (chapter 4); student development (chapter 5); curriculum development (chapter 6); community, economic, and workforce development (chapter 7); staff development (chapter 8); and resource capacity development (chapter 9).

Part III, "Special Strategic Dimensions," covers management strategies for specific situations. Chapter 10 deals with the important issue of managing conflict and forestalling crisis in any area of community college leadership. Chapter 11 is directed toward new community college presidents and features effective first-year strategies. Recent years have witnessed a flood of retirements of community college presidents, and it has been noted that many of the new, incoming presidents experience difficulties during their first year in office. Chapter 11 provides guidance and insight to help new presidents gain confidence and find their voice amid the excitement and challenge associated with their new role.

We assert that community college leaders fail to achieve the preferred future for the community colleges they serve for two reasons:

1. They approach visioning and strategizing in simplistic, linear ways rather than embrac-

ing a strategic framework that responds to the complexity and turbulence of the environment in which community colleges exist today.

2. They fail to align institutional operations to the mission, vision, and core strategies of the college. They do not develop effective execution strategies that provide a roadmap for the faculty and staff as they strive to contribute to achieving the college's preferred future.

This book's unique feature is the focus on execution of core institutional strategies. The key word is *alignment*. This book outlines ways leaders can align areas of execution (policy development, curriculum development, faculty and staff development, community development, financial development, etc.) to the mission, vision, and core strategies of the college. This is applied leadership, and this is what community college leaders do on a daily basis.

Acknowledgments

We acknowledge the support and sponsorship of this book from COMBASE, a national community college consortium for the advancement of community-based, postsecondary education. All the authors are active members of COMBASE. We hope that the mission of COMBASE—to serve as an advocate for community-based education as a central focus of community colleges—is expressed throughout this book. We especially thank the COMBASE executive director, David Pierce, and its board of directors for their support and encouragement.

We are indebted to the many colleagues and mentors who have guided us through our community college careers. Many of the insights contained in this manuscript we learned from them, and now it is our privilege to share these with our readers. We are indebted to the members of the boards of trustees with whom we have worked, as well as our faculty and staff colleagues, who have molded our leadership skills and styles. We think that the best community college presidents are in part the product of the education in leadership they received from their board, faculty, and staff colleagues.

We acknowledge the following individuals for their contributions to the development and production of this book:

Brian Tell, for his editorial services

Donna Carey, former editor, Community College Press, for her guidance and support

Jacqueline Edlund-Braun, acting editor, Community College Press, for being an understanding partner throughout the editing process

Norma Kent, vice president of communications, AACC, for her faith in this project and for her patience

George Boggs, president and CEO, AACC, for his insights that shaped the "instructional" or coaching nature of this manuscript

Part I

A FRAMEWORK FOR LEADERSHIP STRATEGIES

Chapter 1

LEADERSHIP STRATEGIES: AN OVERVIEW

Gunder Myran

The final test of a leader is that he leaves behind him in others the conviction and the will to carry on.

—Walter Lippman, political and social commentator

You certainly have to be a strategist, but you'd better make sure that you are involved in the orchestration, the implementation of strategy as well. If you don't, and it doesn't succeed, you're toast.

—Larry Bossidy (2002)

In this chapter I introduce a new definition of strategic leadership for the community college. Here, *strategy* is defined as an integrated and holistic set of decisions that charts the future course of the college and creates the institutional environment for the successful execution of the strategy. Strategy here is seen not as a single beacon in the future, but rather as a framework within which the major development themes of the college are encompassed: the success of students, staff, and community; internal operational excellence; resource alignment and coherence; and institutional learning and growth. On the basis of this definition, *strategic leadership* has both visionary and operational elements; it deals with both strategy and execution.

LINKING STRATEGY AND EXECUTION

Using the analogy of a ship, the renowned organizational strategist Peter Senge once asked, what is the role of the leader? Is he or she the captain at the helm of the ship, the engineer keeping the engines running, or the social director keeping the passengers happy? The answer: none of these. Rather, the leader is the architect of the ship, designing it so that it has all the components it needs to make a successful journey and reach its intended destination. The old image of the community college president (or the chancellor of a multi-college district) as the captain at the helm, the all-seeing leader scanning the horizon and shouting commands to the crew, is being replaced by the image of the president as the architect, the designer of the community college. The president is part of an executive team that includes the leaders of the major components of the college, such as instruction, student services, administration and finance, human resources development, and community development. Together, the president and the other executive team members must combine the artistic and scientific skills of the architect to continuously design the college so that it can achieve its best possible future.

When an architect designs a ship, the design must encompass not only the hull and the superstructure, but also all the operational systems that permit the ship to run smoothly—the steering mechanism, the rudder, the engine specifications, the sleeping and eating arrangements for the passengers and crew, and so on. Likewise, the leaders of a community college must design not only the strategic elements of the organization—the mission statement, the vision statement, and the core strategies—but also the various operational units, systems, and structures that will be used to execute the strategy. The community college executive leads an integrated and holistic decision-making process that not only charts the future of the college but also creates the environment and the capacity to achieve that future.

The linking of strategy and execution becomes clear if we continue the analogy of the ship with specific reference to the bridge. In the past, the president may have been thought of as the only leader capable of setting the course and steering the ship. Today, many leaders, including faculty and staff members, are present on the bridge and participate in steering the college. This is because no one person, no matter how wise or experienced, can possibly scan the environment alone and anticipate all the economic, demographic, and social changes that will have an impact on the college. Furthermore, those who will align the operations of the college to move according to the course set at the helm will be more effective if they share a commitment to the plan.

STRATEGIC CHANGE

Community colleges are distinguished among higher education institutions by their responsiveness to the changing education needs of the community of which they are part. Community colleges are continuously identifying new markets for education services, creating business and other community liaisons, establishing joint ventures, creating forms of vertical integration with high schools and universities, and developing new education products and delivery systems. A scan of the strategic changes taking place in American community colleges indicates an emphasis, with regard to teaching and learning, on the outcomes of learning (effectiveness); workforce education; new modes of instructional delivery, especially distance learning; civic education; global education; and new responses to student diversity. With regard to the success of staff, strategic changes appear to be taking place in leadership development, curriculum development (an expanded role for faculty), and governance and decision making (new approaches to faculty and staff involvement).

These examples demonstrate the dynamic, complex, and exciting environment within which community college leaders work. The success of these major innovations clearly depends on the implementation capacity of various college units and the integration of the strategic and operational decisions that are involved.

Strategic leaders need to understand how the various parts of the organization's system work together, and they must integrate perspectives across the organization. If they don't, they are likely to be frustrated in their attempts to create and accomplish organizational goals, because individuals in the organization won't have a clear perception or understanding of their roles in supporting achieving those goals. (Beatty & Quinn, 2002, p. 4)

THE STRATEGY TEAM

> *Never doubt that a small group of thoughtful, committed people can change the world; indeed, it is the only thing that ever has.*
> —Margaret Mead

The community college governing board and the president form the partnership that ensures that the community college is responsive to the changing education needs of the citizens in the college's service area. Empowered by this partnership, the president and the other members of the executive team become the primary strategists of the community college. This strategy team, in consultation with the board of trustees, makes the pattern of decisions, for good or for ill, that determines the long-term future and direction of the college. The strategy team then guides the development of programs, services, structures, and systems to achieve that future. The executive team members are selected for this unique leadership role on the basis of their maturity, experience, wisdom, and good judgment. Led by the president, the team filters the continuous flood of information and impulses about changes in both the external and internal environments. Their unique role is to anticipate the impact that environmental changes will have on the future of the college, envision the best future for the college in light of these environmental changes, and then create that best future, making it a living reality.

In a world of constant, rapid change and increasing complexity, it is no longer sufficient for the president and the executive team to focus on a single strategy. For example, a college that declares itself a learning college—one focused on students' learning—misses the consideration of other vital strategic areas, such as community development and service. Today, community college leaders must develop a *strategic framework* within which the pattern of decisions in various areas of organizational development can be envisioned and individual decisions can be reviewed, made, orchestrated, and executed. This strategic framework is based solidly on the institution's *foundational statements*, and it in turn serves as the basis for *execution strategies*.

Foundational Statements

Foundational statements indicate the social purpose of the college (why the college exists), the values on which the faculty and staff base their actions and decisions, and the functions through which the mission is achieved (how the mission will be carried out). Components include the following:

- Mission statement: the most enduring statement of the college's social purpose and a crystallized expression of the college's fundamental strategy

- Values statements: a declaration of the beliefs to which the faculty and staff members are committed, which will be expressed in the daily actions and decisions of all those associated with the community college
- Functions statements: definition of the broad functions through which the mission will be achieved
- Service area definition and target student populations (including areas served through distance learning)

Strategic Framework

The strategic framework is the pattern of strategic, institution-level decisions that will shape the development of the college as it seeks to carry out its mission in the context of anticipated external and internal changes within 5 to 10 years. The strategic framework is defined by dimensions such as student success, community success, faculty and staff success, operational excellence, resource alignment and coherence, and institutional learning and growth. It involves the following specific elements:

- Vision statement: a condensed statement of the preferred future that all associated with the college will devote their talents and energies to achieve
- Development of the organizational culture (including decisions about enhancing an organizational culture defined by good communications, teamwork, tolerance of differences, celebration of diversity, honesty, fairness, mutual respect, and valuing of one another)
- Measurement of organizational effectiveness and continuous improvement (including the involvement of citizens, students, faculty, staff, and other key stakeholders in measuring student learning outcomes, community success outcomes, and other yardsticks of institutional effectiveness, and in bringing about continuous organizational improvement based on these measurements)
- Core strategies: decisions about major college development outcomes to be achieved during the next five to ten years

Core strategies describe the intended outcomes in each area of the framework, how the strategies will be implemented, and how success will be measured. If the strategic framework provides the map of the main roadways, and vision provides the destination, then the core strategies outline the exact route to be taken. Some of the core strategies will move the college toward student success or community success, whereas others will focus on faculty and staff success, operational excellence, or institutional learning and growth. Core strategies, then, are decisions about where the college seeks to be within a set time period along the main roadways to its future.

Execution Strategies

Execution strategies are steps taken by various college leaders and units to execute the vision and the core strategies, including annual planning and budget development. Continuing the analogy of the roadmap, execution strategies can be viewed as driving instructions for all units of the college. These instructions are designed to align all the operational functions of the college with the vision and core strategies. In this way, all parts of the college move toward the designated destination in a unified and integrated way. Execution strategies include the following:

- Student success initiatives, including student services development
- Curriculum and program development, including workforce development and continuing education
- Organizational design development, including the administrative structure, the academic structure, faculty and staff involvement and governance structure, and college systems
- Instructional support development, including learning resources and learning technologies
- Community development and area economic development
- Enrollment planning and development
- Policy development and board member development
- Shared services development (bookstore, food service, purchasing, financial services, personnel services, secretarial services, custodial services)
- Resource development, alignment, and coherence (building reputation, image, and good will; financial development; facility and site development; information systems and communication processes development; and staff professional development, including leadership development and labor–management relations development)

An example of an execution strategy may be helpful here. A dimension of the strategic framework of most community colleges is resource development, alignment, and coherence. An important part of this is financial development. Building the college's financial capacity and targeting these resources in a way that maximizes the alignment with institutional strategy is a vital leadership role. The president works with the chief financial officer, the executive team, and other personnel to build the financial capacity of the college, using the following execution strategies: state appropriation requests, federal and state grants, foundation grants, voter approval of millage increases or bonding authorizations, and tuition and fee proposals. The team might also design financial planning, control, and allocation systems that ensure alignment of the institution's financial resources to institutional strategy. Similar examples of execution strategies could be provided in areas such as instruction, student services, and human resources development.

LEADING TRANSFORMATIONAL CHANGE

Thomas Jefferson once said that "every generation needs a revolution." By that, he meant that each generation of citizens needs to be involved in reinventing its government in order to develop a sense of ownership, connectedness, and personal commitment. Likewise, the board of trustees, the executive team, administrators, faculty, students, local community and business leaders, and the citizens of the college's service area need to be involved in a periodic in-depth assessment of the college's mission, values, functions, vision, and core strategies. Given the rapid pace of demographic, economic, social, and political change, experience indicates that this in-depth assessment should take place at community colleges about every three or four years. In this way, new members of the governing board, new faculty and staff, and new community and business stakeholders can develop a sense of ownership, connectedness, and personal commitment based on a shared approach to establishing the strategic directions of the college. At the same time, those having a longer association with the college can reaffirm their shared sense of mission and direction.

A Four-Level Institutional Change Model

The term *transformational change,* when applied to the community college, requires further definition. Imagine a tree and that transformational change involves change in the roots and trunk of the tree—that is, the mission, values, functions, vision, and core strategies of the college. The branches of the tree represent the more specific tactical elements of the strategic plan and the annual action plans and budgets. Based on a four-level institutional change model, transformational change is the fourth and highest level of change in the community college, although all levels of change form part of the strategic framework.

Level-1 change addresses operational aspects that are broken and need immediate fixing. If a library cannot open because the lights are not working, the problem must be resolved immediately. If the registration line is stopped because of a computer system breakdown, the system must be fixed without delay. Institutional services must have the capacity to respond to these immediate needs quickly and effectively. The creation and maintenance of these responsive services is an integral aspect of institutional strategy. The executive team must ensure that the capacity to respond exists and that those in charge have the authority to act immediately.

Level-2 change addresses execution strategies with a focus on operational excellence. At this level, the college has the capacity not only to fix the immediate problems, but also to correct the systems so that they operate effectively in the future. When the computer system fails, for example, the resolution must address the underlying problem so that it does not occur again. When various routine institutional systems, such as admissions, class registration, class schedules, new employee hiring and orientation, payroll, and annual planning and budgeting, operate smoothly, they do so because the executive team has created an environment that empowers unit leaders to develop systems, structures, and staff assignments and competencies that make operational excellence possible. Creating a climate of operational excellence is an integral part of institutional strategy. Operational excellence is the engine for implementing institutional strategy through the day-to-day actions and decisions of faculty and staff members.

Level-3 change deals with future-shaping initiatives that typically appear in the three-year or five-year plan of the college. These initiatives may be referred to as core strategies because they create a route or path to the future along which more specific implementation or execution strategies will be channeled. For example, core strategies that will be aligned to execution strategies may include increasing enrollment from 10,000 to 12,000 students, undertaking the expansion of the college's service area, introducing a new area of curriculum, shifting resource allocations to undertake a major building program, or playing a major role in an economic development initiative in the community. Each core strategy is integrated and unified with the other strategies in the framework. In turn, these core strategies are aligned to execution strategies.

Level-4 change may be referred to as transformational change; that is, change in the roots (mission, functions, values, design, and vision) of the college. A story is told about the members of a native tribe who leave their traditional homeland because of drought. On their journey, they come to a raging river beyond which they can see a desirable future homeland.

Some members want to return to their traditional homeland and make the best of it, and some members suggest that the group could just settle down by the river. However, a few of the most adventuresome members decide to attempt to navigate the river currents. When they are successful, they encourage others to do the same. Slowly, the majority of the members make their way across the river to their new homeland, although a few return to their drought-stricken traditional homeland or settle by the river.

This is a good description of transformational change in the community college. There comes a time in the life of a community college when the typical strategic changes are not adequate to deal with changing community conditions or internal conditions, and when the executive team must lead those associated with the college away from their comfortable programs, services, structures, and systems to reinvent the college. An examination of the activities of American community colleges engaged in transformational change suggests a pattern of initial assessment, followed by dialogue and decision making, yielding solid results, summarized as follows.

Assessment

- In-depth community education needs and workforce trends assessment
- Internal, in-depth assessment of major programs, services, structures, and systems
- Benchmarking of best practices of outstanding community colleges
- Study of institutional climate and culture
- Assessment of the college's learning environments
- Advice from selected community college leaders

Dialogue and Decision Making

- Faculty and staff town meetings
- Community advisory committees
- Student and community focus groups
- Administrative retreats and workshops
- Strategy sessions, workshops, and reports
- E-mail and chat rooms
- Study teams and committees

Results of Transformational Change

- New mission statement
- New values statements
- New functions statements
- Core strategies, including instructional program and learning environment transformation
- Strategic plan outlining core strategies, execution strategies, and measurement of progress
- Annual plan and budget cycle
- Faculty and staff roles update
- New forms of faculty and staff engagement
- Community image and communications enhancement

TRANSLATING STRATEGY INTO OPERATIONAL TERMS

Community college leaders fail because of bad implementation more often than because of bad strategy. They do not sufficiently take into account the ability and capacity of the organization to actually execute the strategy. The achievement of most institutional plans for change will depend in some way on all or most of the execution strategies just listed. For example, the success of a plan to develop the college's role in advanced technology education in the service area will depend on appropriate execution in areas such as curriculum development, faculty and staff professional development, financial development, and facility development. The challenge for the president and the executive team is to make execution decisions in a coherent, integrated, and holistic way that translates the strategy into successful implementation.

It is common to think of the community college president as the person in the center of change—one who has the ability to dream, to anticipate community change, and to imagine the best future for the college. It is less common to think of the president as executing strategy, but that is what effective leaders spend much of their time on. In *The Strategy-Focused Organization*, Kaplan and Norton (2001) illustrated how the president and the executive team engage in execution strategies. They also described the strategy-focused organization as one that aligns its executive teams, business units, human resources, information technology, and financial resources to its organization's strategy. Based on their research in successful strategy-focused organizations, they observed five principles at work.

1. *Translate the strategy into operational terms.* Successful companies engage all employees in implementing the strategy. They use operational terms to describe the strategy and the means of measuring its achievement. They measure intangible outcomes, such as customer satisfaction, as well as traditional financial yardsticks.
2. *Align the organization to the strategy.* The strategies of the various units of successful organizations are linked and integrated, with synergy as the overarching goal. They replace functional isolation with strategic themes that provide a consistent message and set of priorities across units.
3. *Make strategy everyone's everyday business.* The executive team of successful organizations communicates and educates the entire organization regarding the strategy.
4. *Make strategy a continuous process.* Measurement, both qualitative and quantitative, of the achievement of the strategy provides a feedback loop with results known to the entire organization. Strategy meetings and open reporting of results involving a wide spectrum of managers create a sense of ownership and excitement. The leaders of successful organizations use this continuous feedback to constantly fine tune their strategy.
5. *Mobilize change through executive leadership.* Successful organizations foster feelings of ownership within and active involvement of the executive team. Top leaders energetically spearhead the process, requiring change in every part of the organization and promoting teamwork to coordinate these changes. Leaders mobilize change and create momentum. (Kaplan & Norton, 2001, pp. 10–17)

Institutional Example

Presented here are selected elements of the strategic framework contained in the 2000 strategic plan of Washtenaw Community College, Ann Arbor, Michigan. All faculty and staff groups were involved in the creation of these statements.

WCC mission statement: Our college strives to make a positive difference in people's lives through accessible and excellent educational programs and services.

WCC values:

1. Teaching and learning: we embrace teaching and learning as our central purpose.
2. Support: we make every effort to help learners achieve success.
3. Diversity: we respect differences in people and in ideas.
4. Partnerships: we plan and work together with respect, trust, and honesty within the college and with the communities we serve.
5. Innovation: we seek the best possible ways to conduct our work.

WCC functions:

1. Occupational and career education
2. General and transfer education
3. Continuing education and community services
4. Developmental education
5. Student services
6. Community leadership

WCC vision statement: WCC is a learner-centered, open-door college dedicated to student, community, and staff success. We offer a wide spectrum of community college services, with an emphasis on premier technical and career education programs. The college staff continuously learns to improve learning.

Examples of WCC core strategies:

1. Enhance the outcomes of student learning; increase student retention and success in courses and programs.
2. Increase innovation through an integrated and rapid curriculum and program development system.
3. Redesign the "open door" with a focus on helping at-risk and underserved persons get and keep a good job.
4. Nurture Washtenaw County as a learning community.

Examples of WCC execution strategies:

1. Create the Washtenaw Technical Middle College (charter technical high school) on the WCC campus.
2. Create a Job Skills Academy within Student Services.
3. Draw up a technology investment plan; engage faculty in learning technology adaptation.
4. Determine WCC's financial future through a millage increase election.

CONCLUSION

The essence of the daily life of the community college president and other members of the executive team is making and influencing decisions. Together, the president and the executive team, working with the governing board, are charged with making the key decisions that create the strategic framework and chart the future course of the college. Within a general strategic framework of student success, community success, faculty and staff success, operational excellence, resource alignment and coherence, and institutional learning and growth, the college develops core strategies and outlines implementation plans and measurements.

The executive team works to increase the capacity of those with decision-making authority at all levels to make wise decisions that are aligned to the strategic framework and the core strategies. By empowering staff members to work within a zone of authority, the college executives create an environment in which the hundreds of operational decisions that are made each day are linked to the direction of the institution as a whole. To give concrete expression to the mission, vision, and strategic framework of the college, the executive team creates a web of interaction and influence throughout the college. This means that the president may be involved in a curriculum development matter at one meeting, a personnel matter at the next, and a financial matter at the next. However, the common thread running through these activities is the alignment of these operations with the strategic direction of the college as a whole.

A final thought: The successful community college strategist is one who pulls the preferred future into the present, regardless of how different that future is from the status quo. The president and the executive team must at times, to paraphrase Thomas Jefferson, lead an institutional revolution. Beatty and Quinn (2002) stated that "leading strategically often demands courage and the willingness to swim against the tide of conventional wisdom" (p. 4). These are precisely the qualities that can enable a community college president to engage his or her institution in the dynamic process of transformational change. ❖

References

Beatty, K., & Quinn, L. (2002, May/June). Strategic command: Taking the long view for organizational success. *Leading in Action*, 22(2), 4.

Bossidy, L. (2002, June 10). Advice from the top. *USA Today*, p. 48.

Kaplan, R. S., & Norton, D. P. (2001). *The strategy-focused organization*. Boston: Harvard Business School Press.

Chapter 2

ACHIEVING TRANSFORMATIONAL CHANGE

George A. Baker III

The foundation for the concept of transformational leadership requires a vision of change, communication to accomplish that vision, and a means for followers to accomplish that vision through their own commitment to it.

—J.M. Burns (1978)

Over the past 40 years, community colleges have become fully established in the American higher education landscape. They have also been in a state of continual flux as each college—and each successive college leadership team—has set about trying to align its mission with the needs of the community that it serves. Today, community colleges are facing a paradigm shift: from *available* to *convenient,* from *teaching* to *learning,* from *supported* to *self-assisted,* from *insulated* to *community-based,* from *self-focused* to *customer-focused.* This dramatic shift has muddied the path to the future for community college leaders. When faced with widespread and rapid societal changes, leaders often find that mapping the best route for their colleges can be an overwhelming task.

In this chapter, I discuss big picture strategies for reaching transformational change—the fourth level of change described in chapter 1. These strategies speak to the leadership roles of community college presidents and executives in shaping the organizational culture of their colleges. They generally involve a process of institutional self-assessment, a period of in-depth dialogue and decision making, and a set of resulting new or revised statements about mission, values, functions, core strategies, and corresponding operational plans.

College leaders must understand how best to choose and carry out these big-picture strategies, because they ultimately set the stage for success in more specific operational areas, such as student development, curriculum development, and resource development. Organizational culture is the key. By consciously addressing the organizational culture within their institutions, community college leaders may be able to equip their colleges with the skills, energy, and positive morale to respond to changes beyond their control, to implement changes and innovations of their own creation, and to continue to steer toward a future that will uphold their institution's mission, vision, and values.

ASSESSING THE COLLEGE CULTURE

What exactly is organizational culture? If culture is a pattern of assumptions judged as a valid way to perceive, think, and feel, then the organizational culture of an institution such as a community college can be thought of as its personality (Baker & Associates, 1992; Schein, 1992). The organizational culture reflects the college's values, philosophy, norms, and unwritten rules. It has a powerful effect on how members of the organization behave and carry out their responsibilities, because its underlying, often hidden assumptions guide members' actions and influence the way in which the college as a whole processes information.

Understanding the importance of organizational culture is crucial for college leaders who hope to engage their institutions in a process of transformational change. College presidents and their teams must find appropriate leverage points for long-term, large-scale change within their institutions, which can be done only by assessing thoroughly and honestly the organizational culture of their institutions. In the following paragraphs, I describe some methods and tools that can be used for making such an assessment.

The College Life Cycle

Colleges can be said to move through life cycles similar to those of biological organisms. They experience stages of birth, growth, maturity, decline, and revitalization. By examining what types of processes are important in each stage, one might identify in advance what are the possible types of behavior, demands, and constraints for the president and the leadership team at a given point in time. In terms of college transformation, this would mean that col-

Table 2.1	The Community College Life Cycle
Birth	• Participative process for developing college vision, securing resources, long-range strategic planning • Staffing is significant challenge • Purchase and/or development of management, information, personnel, central, and reward systems • Some conflicts with collective bargaining units, personnel organizations re: workloads, conditions of work, and performance/reward systems • Strong legislative support
Growth	• Focus on internal demands such as staffing, motivation, organization and work design, resource allocation, and coordination • Continued strong legislative support
Maturity	• Focus on performance excellence, accountability and quality of programs and systems • Shifting legislative expectations and levels of support
Decline	• Focus on managing rapidity/scale of growth and changes; performance, accountability, and quality demands become overwhelming • Original pool of faculty and staff begin to retire; tight labor market poses challenges to attracting/retaining good faculty and staff • Competitive pressures felt from other colleges, universities, and proprietary vocational training institutions • Legislative support wanes
Revitalization	• Often characterized by change in leadership—either president, board of regents, or both
Note. Adapted from Lacoursiere (1980).	

lege leaders could identify their colleges' current stage in the life cycle and use that as a starting point for a deeper assessment of the organizational culture. Table 2.1 illustrates the life cycle that community colleges generally follow.

New (often combined) community colleges are born or reborn each year. At the same time, other community colleges are being terminated by legislative action. Deegan and Tillery (1985) outlined various missions of the community college in different periods of its development, demonstrating how societal and environmental needs have influenced the community college mission.

For example, Cohen and Brawer (1989) cited increased numbers, diversity, faculty, governance, finances, and community education as factors that have intensified the challenges faced by the community college and its leaders. Vaughan & Associates (1983) cited loss of funds, tuition increases, an unclear mission, the quality of programs being offered, and governance as obstacles and frustrations for community college leaders. Yet most community colleges today are resolving their conflicts, areas of dissatisfaction, and related crises and are taking steps to better meet the needs of their learners and their communities. For college leaders, an understanding of the community college life cycle and the place of their institution within it is an important element in achieving such transformational change.

The Professional Bureaucracy

Professional bureaucracies exist wherever professionals such as teachers, professors, engineers, doctors, or nurses control outcomes by working directly with customers. Understanding the nature of the professional bureaucracy within the community college environment is a key to

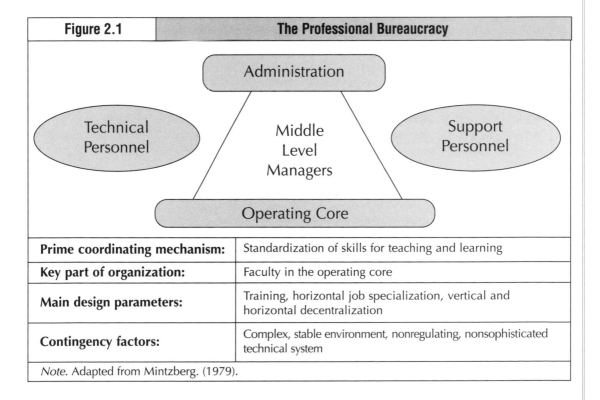

Figure 2.1	The Professional Bureaucracy

Administration

Technical Personnel

Middle Level Managers

Support Personnel

Operating Core

Prime coordinating mechanism:	Standardization of skills for teaching and learning
Key part of organization:	Faculty in the operating core
Main design parameters:	Training, horizontal job specialization, vertical and horizontal decentralization
Contingency factors:	Complex, stable environment, nonregulating, nonsophisticated technical system

Note. Adapted from Mintzberg. (1979).

understanding the organizational culture of these institutions. According to Mintzberg (1979), in professional bureaucracies such as schools and colleges, the operating core is the controlling element in the accomplishment of the organizational mission. The operating core at community colleges is the cadre of full- and part-time faculty and instructors who provide the mission-critical services—that is, teaching, instruction, and facilitation. Figure 2.1 illustrates the shape and design of the professional bureaucracy and outlines its basic structure in a community college.

The work of the faculty as the operating core must be controlled directly by the faculty members who need to exercise some degree of leadership and management to sequence and schedule the work. The operating core also requires an administrative element to maintain continuity, equity, safe environments, and communication, as well as to evaluate the quality of learning delivery systems. Historically, faculty members have employed their collective power to resist changes imposed by the administration.

A major issue today is how teachers teach. Many researchers have argued that with new technology, experiential learning, and improved curricula, teachers will probably be most effective as coaches and facilitators. However, not all teachers agree with the researchers. This is a golden opportunity for community college leaders to create dialogue around the issue of the teaching–learning process.

Learning Histories

To understand, and thus to manage, the organizational culture of their colleges, leaders may need to reconstruct the history of how various college groups and divisions have responded to and solved major problems of adaptation to external conditions and integration of internal issues. The leader must also focus on the kinds of solutions that have repeatedly worked and have become embedded in the culture, so that he or she will be able to draw on them and adjust them to meet new problems and challenges. Many organizational learning experts, such as Peter Senge, George Roth, and Art Kleiner, have advocated the use of a learning history.

Gill defined a learning history as a "highly structured group reflection [that] . . . provide[s] an opportunity to look back on an important event or series of events in the life of the group and to learn collectively from successes and failures" (Gill, 2000). The key benefit of a learning history is the ability to evaluate experiences, whether positive or negative, in a way that helps key stakeholders move beyond them to share a vision that can give rise to new action plans.

LEADERSHIP STRENGTHS

Although community college presidents must concern themselves with the day-to-day management of college operations, essentially their role is to make decisions and to set the tone for how others make decisions. If they are to successfully engage their institutions in the process of transformational change, community college leaders must possess and be able to draw on a variety of management skills and competencies. The Leadership Competencies Assessment Instrument (LCAI), based on the work of Mintzberg and others, is intended to measure the managerial competencies of community college presidents. The LCAI groups 12 managerial roles under 3 categories: Leadership, Informational, and Decisional. Table 2.2 presents descriptions of each of these managerial roles, drawn from surveys conducted with community college presidents.

Athans (2000) employed the LCAI to study 118 community college presidents who were members of the American Association of Community Colleges (AACC), presided over single stand-alone campuses of fewer than 5,000, and answered to a local governing board. The presidents were asked to indicate their perceived level of competency (on a scale of 5 to 1, with 5 being highest) in each of the managerial roles. Competency was defined as a "natural or acquired facility in a specific certainty" (Baker & Associates, 1999). They gave themselves the highest ratings in the "leadership" roles of visionary and ambassador, in the "informational" role of advocate, and in the "decisional" roles of change agent and negotiator.

These results indicate the importance of the community college president's role in envisioning, advocating, and engaging in the institutional process of transformational change.

Table 2.2	Descriptions of Managerial Roles
Role	**Characteristics**
Leadership	
Ambassador	• Presides at official functions as a symbol of the college or as a symbol of external groups and organizations • Promotes goodwill and commitment between the organization and its stakeholders
Visionary	• Thinks globally • Considers future possibilities • Recognizes momentum • Applies convictions about education • Applies concepts about quality
Liaison	• Develops collaborative relationships with groups or individuals in and out of the college service area • Establishes a close bond between the organization and its customers or partners
Motivator	• Establishes mutual trust • Encourages creative and innovative performance • Increases job satisfaction • Rewards people appropriately • Manages individual and organizational stress
Task Giver	• Defines and structures roles for followers • Provides direction • Defines standards • Is biased toward taking action but is flexible • Has high expectations • Uses authority properly
Informational	
Advocate	• Keeps various segments of the community informed of the organization's progress in fulfilling its mission • Deals effectively with mass media • Has a working knowledge of federal, state, and local political processes

Table 2.2	Descriptions of Managerial Roles (Cont'd)
Role	**Characteristics**
Informational	
Monitor	• Assesses the needs of the institution and uses them to identify programs and services • Evaluates opportunities • Develops and analyzes policy • Understands the informal organization • Employs technology to support decision making • Facilitates development and maintenance
Disseminator	• Makes use of technology • Uses effective techniques for speaking, writing, listening, and reading • Makes effective use of formal and informal communications • Coordinates various functions within the organization • Identifies talent in staff members • Develops a personnel performance appraisal process
Decisional	
Change Agent	• Sets measurable objectives • Develops strategies, plans, and quality initiatives • Makes prudent decisions • Designs plans • Provides motivation for change • Seeks new opportunities
Disturbance Handler	• Identifies problems and works to resolve them • Finds alternatives to produce win–win outcomes • Resolves conflict and other problems to the satisfaction of those involved
Negotiator	• Represents the institution in major and local negotiations • Is skilled in and has a working knowledge of group dynamics, conflict resolution, decision making, and problem solving

Note. Descriptions are based on a survey using the Leadership Competencies Assessment Instrument. Roles are presented in descending order of assigned importance by survey participants. Liaison and Motivator received equal scores in the survey.

American community college presidents today fill many of the same roles as they did 10 or 20 years ago. I believe, however, that the roles of change agent, negotiator, visionary, and ambassador are growing both in terms of importance and in the amount of time presidents spend in each. The more aware college leaders are of the relative importance of each of their managerial roles, the better they can adjust the roles of the executive team to complement the president's role. For example, if the external requirements of the ambassador role require the president to devote more time to activities in the community and with the board, the other members of the executive team should be prepared to provide additional influence in the other roles that the president has traditionally performed. In this way, an institution can proceed through the process of major institutional change without undue disruption to ongoing management concerns.

BECOMING A LEARNING ORGANIZATION

Transformational change in community colleges today is often intended to transform the colleges into learning organizations. Becoming a learning organization means to place learning first in every policy, program, and practice of the college. Applied to community colleges, this is often called the learning college.

Community college presidents and their executive teams should strive to embed the learning college concept, as expressed by O'Banion (1997, 1999) and others, in the organizational culture of their institutions. In this way, leaders will find it easier to convince faculty, staff, and first-line supervisors of the importance of infusing learning into their teaching, leading, and managing efforts, and to enlist their support in the process of transformational change.

The learning college concept involves several key management issues:

- *Monitoring of operations, results, environments, and clients for evidence of the adequacy of the overall performance of the college.* The emphasis on evidence is consistent with recent trends among regional accreditation agencies as the agencies changes their methods of evaluating institutions for initial accreditation or accreditation renewal.
- *Identification of situations that lead to problems and the best means of solving problems by altering college rules, strategies, routines, and goals*
- *Measurement of substantive change through learning competencies, talents, skills, and an increased capacity to adapt to future change* (Boggs, 1998). This is a departure from a narrow view of learning, represented by graduation rates, enrollment persistence, and employment rates. The learning organization concept calls for college personnel to grasp a larger picture of education that includes "rich conversations about the definitions of learning that goes beyond institutional effectiveness data" (O'Banion, 1999, p. 5). Learners are provided opportunities for learning primarily through interactions with one another in teams, groups, and individual development. Professional development, in all its forms, can be viewed as activation points in discussions that incorporate values, morals, and mores pertinent to becoming an educated and competent person.
- *Engagement of all organizational learners as full partners in change processes.* Organizational learners include students, staff, faculty, and trustees. Being full partners in the change process means that all the organizational learners assume primary responsibility for choices.

GAUGING THE COMPETITIVE ENVIRONMENT

As community colleges have matured, they have become comfortable with customary ways in which they serve students and communities. The appeal of tradition is easily understood. However, to meet today's needs and tomorrow's demands, faculty and staff must be prepared to recapture the excitement and passion of the early growth years of their institutions.

Responding to current demands and looking to the future, some colleges have developed a host of new skill certifications, replacing technical degrees. Others have partnered with universities or have developed their own four-year, applied-degree programs. Many colleges have developed degree programs and skill certification training via the Internet. International education, global development, and the current competitive educational environment are forcing community colleges to become educational enterprises. Unfortunately, traditionalists at all levels often resist these and other innovative services.

Astute leaders, however, should take any step and go to any length to build upon tradition while adjusting and changing the college to meet current and future needs of the marketplace. They continuously monitor and evaluate their communities' needs and their colleges' responses to those needs. Such executives are truly transformational leaders, attuned to the strengths, weaknesses, threats, and opportunities that face their colleges. They understand that their colleges operate in an increasingly competitive environment and are aware of their institution's rivals.

To assess the competitive environment, and to gauge the perceptions of college personnel about the need for change, community college leaders often make use of a SWOT (strengths, weaknesses, opportunities, and threats) analysis. Conducting a SWOT analysis is a reflective exercise that explores in depth the question: "If I were to compete with our college (or our department or division), what would I do?" A SWOT analysis should be conducted regularly—for example, annually or every six months—and the results tracked over time by the executive team to highlight trends in the perceptions of competition and change. The results of a typical community college SWOT analysis are shown in Table 2.3.

Table 2.3	Community College SWOT Analysis
Strengths • Relatively secure budget • Staff • Public support • Some degree programs meeting goals and objectives • Organizational learning efforts • College positively affects thousands of people • College recognized as quality provider of degrees and certificates	**Opportunities** • Lots of things to take advantage of • Right conditions, new trustee chair, new CEO of state higher education board • Creation of new curricula and learning opportunities • Boundary issues can be resolved • Improvements in quality in program offerings and student services
Weaknesses • Faculty, staff dissatisfaction • Bureaucratic roadblocks and delays • Lack of planning • Complacency • No measure of value added in programs and services • E-learning offerings not 100% functional	**Threats** • Legislative demands/roller coasters • Budget revisions • Negative public perceptions of some degrees and programs • Competition from other colleges, especially for-profits • Views of new state higher education board CEO not known • Complacency • No changes in enrollments over past few years • Loss of reputation in region • Staff dissatisfaction • New/pace of technology development

Note. Adapted from Bryson (1995, p. 6).

A particularly interesting characteristic of SWOT analyses, as Bryson (1995) empha-sized, is that

> . . . strengths and weaknesses [or opportunities and threats] are often highly
> similar to one another. That is, an organization's greatest strengths may
> also be its greatest weaknesses. . . . Strategic planning team members
> should not be surprised to see such relationships. . . . The trick is to take
> advantage of the strengths and opportunities without being disadvantaged
> by the related weaknesses and threats.

A SWOT analysis can be further divided into internal and external threats and opportuni-ties, and it can be analyzed in terms of the past, present, or future. Moreover, it can be used within many other, larger strategic planning or performance improvement models.

Two examples of institutions that have used SWOT analysis illustrate the role it can play in the process of effecting transformational change. Although these two institutions did not necessarily use the SWOT tool described here, they did analyze strengths, weaknesses, opportunities, and threats.

Institutional Examples

When a new president arrived at Rio Salado College in Arizona in 1990, she faced a college in transition and instituted a series of management models to address the evolving status of the institution. The innovative 12-year-old college, which emphasized instructional technolo-gy and an entrepreneurial attitude, was facing declining enrollments, increased competition from other recently opened colleges, and a reputation as "a college of second choice." The president encouraged the college to adapt Total Quality Management (TQM), a management philosophy that emphasizes meeting and exceeding customer expectations, reducing error, empowering employees and teams, continuous and incremental improvement, prevention, and using tools and data to solve problems. The idea was well received and was implemented over the next few years with significant involvement from all members of the college.

However, by 1994, it became apparent that the TQM process had become bureaucra-tized and incapable of fast, responsive innovation. The college's leaders looked for a new model that would better respond to their current situation, and found their answer in Senge's less structured concept of the learning organization. . . . Although it is difficult to establish a definite cause and effect relationship between the adopted management models and outcomes, Rio increased its full-time student equivalent enrollment by more than 50% between 1990 and 1997.

Phoenix College experienced similar success. Once again, a new president arrived, and found both strengths (a high standard for college teaching, a student-centered culture, and an attractive physical plant) and problems (significant enrollment drop since the prior year; the need for capital for infrastructure improvements; stagnant program development; and a cam-pus climate described as risk-averse, lacking in trust, and low in creativity). Enrollment prob-lems were addressed through renewed outreach and a re-energized business and industry train-ing operation. In 1994, the district succeeded in passing a $386 million bond for rebuilding the campus plant infrastructure and updating the instructional and administrative equipment.

The campus climate issues were more difficult to assess and improve. The president worked to change the campus from a static, hierarchical, paternalistic model to an "interactive organization.". . . The president communicated regularly with faculty and staff through e-mail and invited comments and reactions. Open campus discussions on a variety of strategic topics were held for faculty and staff, and the information gathered was used as part of the strategic planning process. Process improvement teams, composed of faculty and staff, were initiated to look at areas as diverse as custodial services and financial aid. The president met with each team to establish parameters and purposes and to discuss findings and suggestions. Recommendations from these teams have resulted in changes in financial, programmatic, technological, and hiring policies. (Kozeracki, 1998)

CONCLUSION

In leading their colleges through a period of transformational change, strong community college leaders will spearhead the process:

- They will constantly search for better methods to serve their learners and their communities.
- They will develop the institutional will to implement those methods.
- They will convince their employees to adopt this same attitude of continuous improvement.

References

Athans, S. (2000). *Temperament and competency in managerial roles of community college presidents.* Unpublished doctoral dissertation, North Carolina State University, Raleigh.

Baker, G. A., III, & Associates. (1992). *Cultural leadership: Inside America's community colleges.* Washington, DC: Community College Press.

Baker, G. A., III, & Associates. (1999). *Administrative concepts and theories in the public sector.* Raleigh: North Carolina State University.

Boggs, G. (1998, January/February). Accepting responsibility for student learning. *On the Horizon: The Strategic Planning Resource for Education Professionals, 6*(1), 5.

Bryson, J. M. (1995). *Strategic planning for public and nonprofit organizations.* San Francisco: Jossey-Bass.

Burns, J. M. (1978). *Leadership.* New York: Harper & Row.

Cohen, A. M., & Brawer, F. B. (1989). *The American community college* (4th ed.). San Francisco: Jossey-Bass.

Deegan, W., & Tillery, D. (1985). *Renewing the American community college.* San Francisco: Jossey-Bass.

Gill, S. J. (2000). *The manager's pocket guide to organizational learning.* Amherst, MA: HRD Press.

Kozeracki, C. (1998, November). *Managing organizational change in the community college.* Los Angeles: ERIC Clearinghouse for Community Colleges. (ED424884)

Lacoursiere, R. B. (1980). *The life cycle of groups: Group development stage theory.* New York: Human Services Press.

Mintzberg, H. (1979). *The structuring of organizations.* Englewood Cliffs, NJ: Prentice-Hall.

O'Banion, T. (1997). *A learning college for the twenty-first century.* Phoenix: Oryx Press.

O'Banion, T. (1999). *Launching a learning centered college.* Mission Viejo, CA: League for Innovation in the Community College.

Schein, E. H. (1992). *Organizational culture and leadership* (2nd ed.). San Francisco: Jossey-Bass.

Senge, P. M., & Schein, E. H. (1990). *The fifth discipline: The art and practice of the learning organization.* New York: Doubleday.

Vaughan, G., & Associates (Eds.). (1983). *Issues for community college leaders in a new era.* San Francisco: Jossey-Bass.

Chapter 3

STRATEGIC ELEMENTS OF ORGANIZATIONAL DESIGN

Gunder Myran

Had I been present at the creation, I could have given some useful hints
for the better ordering of the universe.

—Alfonso X (1221–1284)

Most faculty and staff members could give some useful hints for the better ordering of their community college. They see institutional strategies fail because of role confusion, inadequate communication between college units, and lack of involvement on the part of those who will be affected by the strategy. These are failures of organizational design. As Goold and Campbell stated: "For most organizations, organizational design is neither a science nor an art, it is an oxymoron. Organizational structures rarely result from systematic, methodical planning. Rather, they evolve over time, in fits and starts, shaped more by politics than policies" (2002, p. 117).

It is probably the case at most community colleges that elements of organizational design, such as the administrative structure, the academic structure, and the governance and decision-making structure, do indeed evolve over time, in fits and starts, shaped more by politics than policies. Yet an effective and current organizational design is vital to the accomplishment of the core strategies of the community college, and the continuous improvement of the design in response to changing community needs and internal changes is a crucial aspect of strategic leadership.

DEFINITION OF ORGANIZATIONAL DESIGN

Organizational design is defined as the architecture of the college—its structures and systems—that serves as a conduit for the achievement of strategy. The design elements of the college are a necessary intermediary between the strategic framework, which is the driving force, and the execution strategies, which can be carried out only through the design elements. Organizational design includes several key elements:

- Administrative structure
- Academic and curricular structure

- Structure of divisions, departments, and offices
- Governance and decision-making structure
- College systems
- Job descriptions for faculty and staff

Designers of the community college exist at every level (e.g., deans, directors, and department chairs), but the chief designers are the president and the executive team members. The objective of community college designers is to design the college so that it has the capacity to implement its core strategies. Capacity involves areas such as curricular design, student services design, the knowledge and skills of faculty and staff, financial resources, information resources, structures, and systems. The designer views the organization as a whole and seeks to create synergy between the various units, structures, and systems of the college. Ultimately, the designer seeks to match the educational outcomes sought by the students, businesses, and communities served by the college with the capacity of the college to deliver those outcomes. Unlike the designer of the college buildings, who produces a relatively static product, the designer of the community college as an organization must create a dynamic and adaptive architecture that can continuously improve programs, services, structures, and systems in response to changing educational needs of the surrounding community.

DESIGN PRINCIPLES

Design principles serve as the conceptual foundation of community college organizational design. In continuously working to improve the structures and systems of the college, the designer benefits from having a beacon, a conceptual target toward which design improvements are directed. An effective design, then, should give life to these principles:

- Whole systems thinking: recognizing the relationships between college functions and leveraging changes based on the dynamics of the whole organization
- Vision and goal orientation: a focus on the future of the college
- Institutional effectiveness: fostering an emphasis on increasing the outcomes of student, community, and staff learning
- Continuous quality improvement: nurturing the continuous improvement of college programs, services, structures, and systems based on measurement of the outcomes of student learning, community success, and staff success
- Customer service: continuous input from students, businesses, and community customers
- Trend analysis and environmental scanning: continuous assessment of local, regional, state, national, and global trends and conditions that may have an impact on the future of the college
- Team-based and participative culture: movement toward leading and managing the college through teams
- Student flow: involvement of all college units in continuous improvement directed toward an increase in student learning, satisfaction, and success at all stages of the student's progress through college programs, services, and systems
- Rapid curriculum and service development: increased speed of curricular and service development

Vertical and Horizontal Design

Vertical design refers to the hierarchical elements of the college design, such as the administrative structure, the academic structure, and the departments, divisions, and offices of the college. Horizontal design refers to the cross-functional teams, interdisciplinary committees, and college-wide systems that cut across the traditional hierarchical structure. Along with growing awareness of the need for colleges to be more adaptive in response to rapidly changing community needs, a shift is taking place from a reliance on the traditional vertical design to an increased emphasis on the horizontal design. This is a positive development, because most challenges faced by colleges are interdisciplinary and cross-functional in nature.

Vertical Design

When most people hear the words *organizational design*, they think of the formal administrative structure. They think of the boxes in which titles of positions are listed and the lines that indicate reporting relationships. The administrative structure is an important design element. It is referred to as the vertical design because it is hierarchical in nature and has the tendency to put people into "silos" where they communicate upward to their supervisor and downward to those who report to them. Individuals in these silos tend to put the objectives of their silo ahead of the objectives of those in other parts of the organization; indeed, they may be unaware of the objectives of other units. When the units in one hierarchical silo communicate with another silo, the message typically goes up the silo, across to the top of the other silo, and then down to the unit for which it was intended.

This method of communicating is very slow and cumbersome and is not suited to the quick-response demands of today's society. For these reasons, some community colleges have experimented with eliminating the hierarchical design and transforming themselves through the adoption of a team-based horizontal design. For most community colleges, however, the hierarchical vertical design will continue to be a standard feature, existing simultaneously with an expanded horizontal design. In that case, the college leadership must periodically evaluate the effectiveness of the administrative structure and revitalize it so that it is responsive to changing internal and external environments.

In the same way, the overall academic–curricular structure and the department–division–office structure should be periodically assessed and revitalized. In the case of the academic–curricular structure, some community college leaders undertake benchmarking exercises by which they compare their institutional structure to those of colleges having exemplary academic programs. Others invite a team of community college academic specialists to conduct an in-depth evaluation of the academic–curricular structure and make recommendations for change. It is also possible to use the Malcolm Baldrige Award or other institutional assessment processes for this purpose.

In an enhanced vertical design, the success of each unit must be defined by its contribution not only to the success of its silo, but also to the success of other silos and to the welfare of the organization as a whole. Supervisors must encourage employees to serve on cross-functional teams and should reward them for having a customer-service orientation. In the case of shared services (human resources, plant operations, security, financial services, computer and information services, institutional research, and planning), most of the customers are internal faculty and staff. The same emphasis on customer service should be expected for units having only internal customers as for units that serve student, business, and community constituencies.

Horizontal Design

Horizontal design refers to the cross-functional teams and systems that function between the boxes on the organization chart. Rummler and Brache described horizontal design as "managing the white spaces between the boxes":

> In our experience, the greatest opportunities for performance improvement often lie in the functional interfaces—those points at which the baton is passed from one department to another. A primary contribution of a manager is to manage interfaces. The boxes already have managers; the senior manager adds value by managing the white space between the boxes. (Rummler & Brache, 1995)

Community college leaders manage the white spaces between the boxes by bringing together staff members from various units to take on cross-functional or interdisciplinary projects or problems. This approach offers several advantages over vertical design. First, most projects and problems are cross-functional in nature, and can best be addressed through shared effort among the relevant offices. Second, people in parallel positions in different offices can work together to solve problems without the delay associated with moving questions and ideas up and down the hierarchy. Third, employees learn as they interact with those from other units, to the benefit of the individuals and units involved as well as the college as a whole. Finally, the teams are more efficient because those with the expertise needed are sitting around the team table rather than isolated in various offices around the college.

There is, of course, great variety in the types of cross-functional teams that now exist in community colleges. Consider the following examples:

- District-wide and college-wide leadership teams, such as the president's (or chancellor's) cabinet
- Curriculum development committees (including program cluster teams for areas such as business careers, technology-oriented careers, health and public service careers, university transfer, customized corporate employee training, basic jobs skills education, and developmental education)
- Information systems user teams
- Institutional effectiveness and student success teams
- Facility development teams
- Community service teams
- Accreditation teams
- Employee recognition teams
- Faculty and staff professional development teams
- Councils of multi-college districts, such as the Student Development Council, the Chief Academic Officers Council, the Business Operations Council, and the Public Information Council

Although standing committees are still a central feature of horizontal design, a growing component is ad hoc action teams that are given a charge, conduct the needed study and dialogue, make a recommendation, and then disband. The members of ad hoc action teams can be selected for team membership based on the skills needed for the specific task, whereas members of standing committees must be generalists who deal with a variety of problems and projects. Ad hoc action teams allow for greater flexibility in forming and disbanding and reduce the energy and time that would have to be devoted to the logistics of a large standing committee structure.

COMMUNITY COLLEGE SYSTEMS

The continuous improvement of college systems is an essential part of college design. In many cases, what appears to be a people problem may turn out to be a systems problem. The execution of college strategy often depends on effective systems that make routine those aspects of college operations that can be routinized, allowing more time to address matters requiring creativity and problem-solving skills. These are some of the major community college systems on which leaders place reliance:

- Marketing, student recruitment, and enrollment planning
- Admissions, assessment testing, and student orientation
- Student academic and career planning
- Registration and placement
- Classroom and faculty support (learning resources, bookstore, copy services)
- Instructional program and curriculum development (credit and noncredit)
- Annual planning budget development
- Faculty and staff individual planning and performance review
- Effectiveness (i.e., measurement of student learning outcomes and related continuous improvement processes)
- Environmental scanning and community and workforce needs assessment

The organizational designer is responsible not only for fostering the continuous improvement of these and other college systems, but also for facilitating synergy among the systems. The greater the cross-functionality and productive interaction across the systems, the more effective the institution is likely to be.

CONCLUSION

The designer of the community college sees the college as a system made up of interdependent parts. In turn, the community college itself is a system within systems, because it is a part of larger community, regional, state, and national systems. The designer seeks to create an organizational architecture such that (1) the interdependence between the college and its environment is recognized; (2) the structures and systems of the college facilitate the achievement of its core strategies; (3) there is continuous improvement of the college's structures and systems; (4) faculty and staff are engaged in continuous organizational learning and improvement as they work on cross-functional projects and problems; and (5) the interdependence of the units and systems of the college is recognized, and increased synergy is achieved.

References

Goold, M., & Campbell, A. (2002, March). Do you have a well-designed organization? *Harvard Business Review, 80*(3), 117.

Rummler, G. A., & Brache, A. P. (1995). *Improving performance: How to manage the white space on the organization chart* (2nd ed.). San Francisco: Jossey-Bass.

Part II

EXECUTION STRATEGIES

Chapter 4

STRATEGIC DIMENSIONS OF POLICY DEVELOPMENT

Gunder Myran

Community college trustees invest their time, energy, knowledge, experience, and talents in improving their community college, thereby improving the quality of life of countless communities across the nation, and of the nation itself.

—George B. Vaughan and Iris M. Weisman (1997)

Policy development is the avenue through which the board of trustees of an American public community college expresses its strategic intentions on behalf of the citizens of the college's service area. As the body legally charged with governing the community college for the public good, the board serves as an agent and advocate of the public by guiding the affairs of the college in ways that ensure that it is responsive to the higher education and workforce development needs of the citizens, businesses, and communities that it serves. In this context, *policy* may be defined as the governing principles, regulations, and direction-setting guidelines established by the board of trustees to guide the operations of the college. Based on this broad definition, applicable state and federal laws become policies of the college, as well as negotiated contracts with labor groups and other agreements that bind the college to a set of actions.

Through its policy-setting role, the board of trustees creates a framework or context within which the president and the executive team, as well as the faculty and staff, make decisions and operate on a day-to-day basis. The board defines what shall be done from a policy perspective, and the president is charged with determining how policies will be executed.

THE STRATEGY-TO-EXECUTION CONTINUUM

The strategy-to-execution continuum with regard to policy development is summarized as follows:

1. The board of trustees, with the advice of the president, establishes policies to guide and regulate the overall development and operation of the organization.
2. The president prepares two types of statements that relate to policy development. The first consists of the president's guidelines, sometimes referred to as "administrative memoranda," that instruct the faculty and staff regarding expectations as to the culture and operations of the college. For example, these memoranda may deal with the expectations for communication among units, the decentralization of decision making,

changes in the administrative structure, or the commitment to continuous quality improvement processes. These memoranda may be seen as a part of the policy manual because they complement board policy in defining the broad administrative parameters within which the college will operate.

3. The second type of document prepared by the president details operational procedures. Linked to board policies, operational procedures specify how the policies will be executed by the faculty and staff. These procedures are typically developed within the college's administrative and governance structure in parallel to the preparation of recommendations to the board regarding new or revised policies. Although these procedures may be shared with the board as policy recommendations are considered, they are not acted on by the board. In this way, procedures can be changed as conditions change, without the necessity of board action. These procedures are typically contained within the policy manual as an adjunct to the policy statement itself.

The methods used by community colleges to develop policy, president's guidelines, and operational procedures vary widely. Recommendations will most likely arise through the college's team, committee, or council structure, to be finally reviewed by the president's cabinet and approved by the president for submission to the board for action.

GOVERNING DEMOCRACY'S COLLEGE

Winston Churchill once said that democracy is the worst form of government in the world, with the exception of all other forms of government. This statement could well apply to the community college. Community colleges are led by executives who are experienced educators with proven leadership skills, and yet these leaders work under the direction of an elected or appointed board made up of citizens whose primary qualifications are an interest in public service and an appreciation of the value of the community college to their community. These trustees may be businesspeople, homemakers, teachers, bankers, health care workers, social workers, lawyers, or members of other professions or occupations, and they are unlikely to have any experience in higher education management.

How then does it make sense that the professional managers are directed by the citizen board members? It makes sense because the community college is the people's college—democracy's college. The people, through their elected or appointed board, "own" the college. (In legal terms, the board of trustees is the owner of the college in most instances, but board members serve on behalf of the community they represent.) The community, not the professional managers or the faculty, determines what the college does in response to changing community needs. Thus, a governing structure that may seem unworkable to outsiders is, in fact, the best possible governing structure for community colleges in a democratic society.

THE BOARD–PRESIDENT PARTNERSHIP

A common theme in community college literature is the delineation of the policy development role of the board and the policy implementation or executive role of the president. It is said that the best test of whether the board is playing its policy role rather than interfering in the management of the college is to take the blood pressure of the president. No doubt the same could be said for the board chair in cases where the president is overstepping his or her limits in terms of policy development. For the college to be successful and moving toward its best future, a strong and positive relationship between the board and the president is essential. The president must nurture many vital relationships—with the faculty, the college staff, community and business leaders, and legislators and government officials—but the most empowering is (or should be) the relationship with the board of trustees.

The board–president relationship is a complex one; it is not simply a boss–employee relationship. The president, as an experienced community college professional, must be able to be a mentor to new board members, and must be able to have dialogue with the board chair regarding the functioning of the board. The president must be able to play a primary role in recommending policies to the board; policy initiatives that arise during a board meeting without adequate study and deliberation by staff are likely to cause confusion and miscues. The president must have the freedom to implement policies and provide for the day-to-day strategic leadership of the college without undue board involvement. Above all else, there must be a relationship of trust between the board and the president. It is impossible to avoid a gray area between the board policy role and the president's executive role, and it is in this gray area that board–president dialogue and mutual trust become so important.

To nurture their vital partnership, the board and the president sometimes agree on a set of shared expectations that might take the following form. Board members have a right to expect that the president will

- Treat all board members equally
- Ensure that there will be no surprises
- Keep the board informed of new developments and emerging problems
- Support the board's decisions
- Recognize the achievements and contributions of board members
- Represent individual board members in a positive and supportive way to the public
- Give candid but private assessments of the board's functioning
- Work with the board chair as the primary communication link between the board and the president, while also ensuring that all board members are kept informed of emerging matters
- Maintain neutrality in board elections

Similarly, the president has a right to expect that the board will

- Be sympathetic to and show understanding of the difficulty and complexity of carrying out the presidential leadership role amid the sometimes conflicting expectations of students, faculty, staff, and the general public
- Support the president in implementing board policy regardless of the outcome of the board vote
- Seek the president's recommendation on policy matters before action is taken
- Inform the president of questions or concerns received from students, faculty, staff, or citizens so that prompt action can be taken, rather than having individual board members attempt to resolve such problems
- Insist that employees use established staff–board communications channels

STRATEGIC ROLES OF THE BOARD OF TRUSTEES

The strategic roles of the local community college board of trustees vary from state to state depending on the state-level structure. In some states, there is a strong state-level leadership structure, including a state community college board. The result may be a more limited role for the local community college board, which may simply be called an advisory committee. In other cases, the state-level structure is more modest, and the role of the local community college governing board is stronger.

If the board of the local community college has sufficient authority to govern the affairs of the institution, it will have two major strategic roles: (1) involvement in determining the college's mission, values, functions, vision, and core strategies in ways that communicate the powerful engagement of the board in shaping the future of the college; and (2) establishing rules and regulations that govern the college in a way that represents the best interests of the student, business, and community constituencies being served.

The Board's Role in Shaping the Future of the Community College

The board's first strategic role, that of powerful engagement in shaping the future of the college, is enacted in a variety of ways. The board of trustees of the Maricopa Community College District in Arizona hosts "strategic conversations" that involve all the key internal and community stakeholders who will be affected by a strategic initiative that is being considered by the district. Many community colleges hold retreats to address strategic directions under consideration. For example, a "student success" retreat may be held to explore policies and core strategies designed to infuse the assessment of student learning outcomes and continuous academic improvement into the college culture. Similarly, a "community success" retreat might explore with community and business leaders new ways the college might be involved in workforce development, economic development, civic education, and multicultural initiatives in the community. In these and other ways, the board gains insights that can influence the future of the college. The board then participates in developing the documents and statements that articulate the strategic decisions and give shape and substance to these insights.

Foundational statements. Covering mission, values, and functions, foundational statements are the most enduring testimony of the social purpose and roles of the community college, and they should be changed only with great care. These statements are the anchors to which college units can tie themselves with some predictability and assurance of stability. The decision to change foundational statements should be the result of careful consultation with all the internal and community stakeholders. Furthermore, these statements should evolve through consensus, because they are most powerful when there is a shared sense of ownership and commitment to what is decided. Stakeholders should be able to see their personal ideals for the college reflected in these foundational statements. For official and documentation purposes, however, these statements should be acted on by the board of trustees.

If there is one area in which the board should play a more directive role, it is in establishing the functions of the community college. Community colleges universally adopt the five basic functions of community colleges (occupational and technical education, university transfer and general education, developmental/remedial education, continuing education, and student services), but the description of these functions should be uniquely stated for each community, based on the local educational needs. The board should also consider whether to add a sixth function now adopted by some community colleges: that of community development or community leadership. By doing so, the board makes a strategic declaration that the college will be a partner with other community agencies in advancing the quality of life in the communities being served.

Vision statement and core strategies. The vision statement is the crystallized expression of the preferred future of the college. The board should play a central role in ensuring that the vision statement expresses the hopes and dreams of those in the community. The vision statement should be reviewed and revised from time to time, based on changing community demographic, social, and economic conditions. As with the foundational statements, the vision statement should be developed through consensus among the key stakeholders and then acted on by the board.

Core strategies turn the vision into action, providing the roadmap for achieving the college's mission and vision during a set period of the institution's development. Here, the momentum of development shifts to the president and the executive team, who will engage the college community in study and dialogue leading to the determination of a set of recommendations on core strategies to be presented to the board. This recommendation may take the form of a strategic plan update. In response to the complexity and rapid change that characterize their service areas, some community colleges are making the change from a formal strategic plan to a strategic framework that is open to continuous change.

The Board's Role in Making Policy Decisions

The second strategic role of the community college board is to act as the owners of the college by making those policy and related decisions that ensure that the college operates in the best interests of the communities being served. Responsibilities include the following:

- Establish, with the advice of the president, policies to govern the affairs of the college
- Select the president when a vacancy exists, and give direction to and evaluate the president
- Provide for the oversight of the financial affairs of the college, including the approval of loans, bond issues, and capital outlay contracts under specified conditions
- Act on a monthly financial report from the president
- Act on the annual budget of the college as recommended by the president
- Provide for the annual audit of all college funds
- Act on recommendations of the president regarding new facilities and the renovation of existing facilities, where the cost exceeds an established amount
- Act on the recommendations of the president regarding the purchase and lease of real estate, or any other legal transactions involving the sale or acquisition of property
- Act on the recommendations of the president regarding new instructional programs
- Act on the recommendations of the president regarding the hiring of staff, compensation levels, and other personnel matters
- Authorize the granting of degrees and certificates
- Act on contracts between the college and organized labor groups

A look at some of the typical items that are included in a community college policy manual illustrates the range of governing principles, regulations, and direction-setting guidelines that are enacted by the board of trustees:

- Bylaws of the board of trustees
- Student admissions policy
- Student residency policy
- Student tuition and fee rates
- Policy on credit for prior learning
- Core curriculum policy
- Degree and certificate structure
- Policy on international travel by students
- Student eligibility for extra- and co-curricular activities
- Policy on release of student information
- Policy on student publications
- Student rights and responsibilities
- Affirmative action policy
- Conflict of interest policy (board, faculty, staff)
- Employee assistance program
- Policy on the prohibition of sexual harassment
- Faculty and staff rules of conduct
- Policy on external use of college facilities
- Policy on purchasing goods and services
- Compliance with the Americans with Disabilities Act
- Policy on commercial speech and conduct on college property
- Policy on a drug-free workplace

As a way of organizing the college's policies and clarifying the role of the board of trustees, some community colleges have adapted the Carver Governance Model, developed by a governance design consultant (see Carver & Mayhew, 1997). In this model, board policy is divided into four categories: ends policies, executive limitations policies, governance process policies, and board-linkage policies. The most promising aspect of this model from a strategic perspective is the emphasis on specifying the outcomes or ends to which a policy is addressed. An advantage of the model is the focus on brief, clear policies to replace the lengthy and detailed policies found in some community college policy manuals. Although "executive limitations" policies have the laudable objective of clarifying the roles of boards and presidents, some presidents find them too rigid and prescriptive. Whether the Carver Governance Model is used or not, the board–president dialogue that produces a set of understandings regarding the policy framework to be developed is very valuable.

CONCLUSION

The strategic role of the board of trustees focuses on ensuring that a community college operates in the best interests of the students, businesses, and communities in the service area. The board carries out this role by being powerfully engaged in shaping the future of the college and by making decisions, including the enactment of policies, that are directed toward this community-based result. The board does not *do* the community college's work, but it must ensure that it *is* done (Carver & Mayhew, 1997, p. 25).

References

Carver, J., & Mayhew, M. (1997). *A new vision of board leadership: Governing the community college*. Washington, DC: Association of Community College Trustees.

Vaughan, G. B., & Weisman, I. M. (1997). *Community college trustees: Leading on behalf of their communities*. Washington, DC: Association of Community College Trustees.

Chapter 5

STUDENT DEVELOPMENT

Beverly Simone

We are in the business of changing lives.

—from a mission statement adopted July 17, 2000, by Montgomery College Board of
Trustees, Montgomery County, MD

Student development at community colleges can be defined as an interwoven set of services, programs, and supports intended to help students succeed while they are enrolled
at the college and after they leave. The Web site of the National Council on Student
Development (www.nationalcouncilstudentdevelopment.org), an affiliate council of the
American Association of Community Colleges, includes the following elements in its
description of student development:

- Enrollment management: recruitment, admissions, retention, and completion
- Mission: transfer, job placement, and multiculturalism
- Academic support services: records, advising, financial aid, disabilities, and orientation
- Student events and activities: student government, publications, organizations, and athletics
- Discipline and grievances
- Service learning
- Health services and insurance
- Counseling
- Safety and security

Each of these is an important aspect of student development. This chapter focuses on four
strategic areas of student development that are especially in need of strong leadership from
community college presidents and their executive teams: learning about educational offerings
and activities, access to programs and courses, student development in the learning environment; and exploration of careers and further education. These areas present student development challenges for community colleges, particularly as college leaders come to grips with the
changing demographics of community college students. (Who are the students? What are their
expectations for what colleges can and should offer? How do they want to access college programs and services?) These areas also present real opportunities for college leaders to ensure
that their institutions offer high-quality services, programs, and experiences that support the
positive psychological, emotional, and intellectual development of all students.

As described in chapter 1, student development is among the core components of a college's foundational strategies (i.e., service area and target populations), strategic framework (citizen/student involvement in defining student learning outcomes), and execution strategies (e.g., deployment of learning resources and technologies to support student access, enrollment, and achievement). This chapter will highlight some key strategies, tools, and resources employed by leading community colleges to create a college environment in which student support is an integrated, essential part of a college's strategic leadership framework—its administrative policies, learning programs, and, most important, the daily practice of staff and faculty. The chapter closes with a brief discussion of some important emerging issues. To provide the contextual framework for the use of strategies, tools, and resources, it is important to review two of the major theories of student development and how they have influenced the present state of student development policies and programs.

Two Theories of Student Development

In *Education and Identity,* Chickering (1969) outlined seven "development vectors" related to traditional college-age students (defined as 18 to 25 years old):

1. *Developing competence* intellectually, physically/manually, and socially
2. *Managing emotions* by becoming aware of feelings, how feelings may affect responses, and how to express feelings
3. *Developing autonomy* by becoming less dependent on the need for affection, reassurance, and approval
4. *Establishing identity* by becoming more aware of physical and sexual self
5. *Freeing interpersonal relationships* through demonstration of increased acceptance and tolerance of differences in others
6. *Developing purpose* through identifying educational and career goals and personal interests
7. *Developing integrity* reflected as a set of values that guide actions

According to Chickering, growth occurs as students encounter and successfully integrate increasingly complex tasks or activities. Growth may occur simultaneously in different vectors and may require repeated exposure. Although growth may occur in different areas at the same time, younger students are more likely to be dealing with the first two or three vectors. As students progress through their college career, they typically work on developing purpose and establishing integrity.

Nancy Merrill, former executive assistant at Madison Area Technical College, has applied the principles of O'Banion's learning college model to student development activities and services; Table 5.1 summarizes how student development may contribute to learning college principles. Merrill's work shows the links between the principles of a learning college and learning activities typically addressed through student services programs and services.

To ensure that all students develop as fully as possible, community college leaders must continually ask how the development activities at their institution affect students of different ages, races, backgrounds, economic conditions, and learning styles. Is the college providing an array of opportunities that will benefit all or most students, or are the activities designed for a particular demographic segment? To address the rapidly changing needs of students, colleges should provide programs and services that represent a holistic approach to student development.

Table 5.1	Correlation Between Learning College Principles and Student Development
Learning College Principles	**Student Development Activities**
Creates substantive change in individual learners	Appropriate placement and advising means students are more likely to be successful in their learning experiences.
Engages learners in the learning process as full partners who assume primary responsibility for their own choices	Recruitment and marketing create student awareness of learning opportunities and options. Learners are responsible for choosing when to enroll and—supported by learning facilitators such as advisers, counselors, and faculty—choosing the types of programs and courses in which to enroll.
Creates and offers as many options for learning as possible	Student organizations and clubs provide new learning experiences. Community or service learning expands learning beyond the classroom, laboratories, and internships. Remedial and developmental courses provide learning options that address individual student needs.
Assists learners to form and participate in collaborative learning activities	Advisers, counselors, and faculty help students identify intern- or externship opportunities.
Defines the roles of learning facilitators by the needs of learners	Enrollment specialists, advisers, counselors, and faculty consider their roles and responsibilities based on student development needs.

Note. Learning college principles are drawn from O'Banion (1997). Student development activities are drawn from Nancy A. Merrill, Madison Area Technical College.

Although awareness of Chickering, O'Banion, and other student development theorists is important, it is appropriate to question the applicability of these theories to the diversity of students in community colleges. For example, which of these theories will yield policies and practices that best serve the student development needs of a 34-year-old mother of two, who is entering college for the first time? Or an engineer with a doctorate seeking to upgrade his computer skills or explore a new career? Or a 16-year-old trying to finish high school and obtain technical college training simultaneously?

Khandi Bourne-Bowie (2000) raised the concern that most theories of student development are "based on Eurocentric world views and have repeatedly failed to adequately address the needs of non-traditional students, including those of African heritage and other students of color" (p. 36). Bourne-Bowie's criticism may have some validity. Besides traditional categories of diversity, such as race and gender, community colleges must consider other areas of difference in our student population:

- Full- or part-time college enrollment
- English as a second language (ESL) needs
- Varying economic status
- Full- or part-time employment status

- Prior higher education experience (college transfer, already possessing a degree)
- Prior workplace education experience
- Daytime, evening, and weekend students
- Distance learners
- Underprepared students

The last item in the list, underprepared students, is an important category today. According to McCabe (2000), in *No One to Waste,* 41% of entering community college students and 29% of all entering college students are underprepared in at least one of the basic skills of reading, writing, or mathematics. Perez (1998) pointed out that current definitions of at-risk students describe the majority of students in American community colleges. How can colleges meet these diverse and challenging needs?

Institutional Example

Educators at New York City Technical College wanted to know if their ESL courses promoted positive academic outcomes within the general curriculum. . . . Comparing the credits earned, matriculation rate, and grade point averages (GPAs) of native-born students to those of new immigrant students showed that immigrant students who initially enrolled in the ESL program tended to have lower GPAs and earned fewer total credits than did native students. These findings may be clouded, however, because they are based on comparison of new immigrants with the mainstream student population rather than with a more comparable subpopulation of English-speaking students enrolled in remediation courses.

Another finding revealed that immigrant students seemed more engaged in the college because they were more likely to take advantage of the various services offered by the institution (e.g., tutoring, counseling, and computer facilities). In addition, immigrant students had a 63% rate of persistence compared to 55% for the native-born students. These data suggested that the ESL program at New York City Technical College led to positive outcomes for new immigrant students. (Kuo, 2000)

Clearly, community college leaders need to have an understanding and awareness of traditional and newly emerging student development theories. The increasing diversity of student populations mandates that we reconsider how we foster student development and even what type of development we should emphasize. Comprehensive student development initiatives must consider the diverse characteristics of the student population and how student development activities can be incorporated into various points of contact with students.

The typical dilemma facing colleges is that how to implement successful student development activities is less clear than what to include as part of student development. One reason for this is the lack of current research on the scope and quality of student services functions in two-year colleges. Mattox and Creamer pointed out that "no national study of two-year college student services has been reported in the literature since 1972" (1998, pp. 3–21). Despite the lack of substantive research in this area, community college presidents and their teams must make daily decisions that affect the quality of student support services. Effective strategies and approaches do exist and are being used by college executive teams to create a holistic student development environment; some of these are described in the next section.

LEARNING ABOUT EDUCATIONAL OFFERINGS AND ACTIVITIES

Each point of contact between a college and its students provides an opportunity to review strengths and weaknesses in student development activities. Starting at the information and recruitment stage, college leaders should ask how potential students learn about the college, its program offerings, and its various support activities. In what ways does the college communicate the breadth and quality of its offerings to the diverse communities of potential students? How early is this information shared? Does the college connect with elementary- and middle-school students? How are senior citizens, underemployed workers, new entrants into the labor force, university students, and others connected with the community college? Do college publications, outreach communications, and media buys appeal to different age and ethnic groups? Are messages communicated in languages other than English?

Answers to these questions will give a community college insight into the varied audiences it is trying to attract or is unintentionally ignoring. Although recruitment may seem beyond the scope of student support and development, in a learner-centered college environment building awareness and attracting students who can benefit from the college are important early stages of ongoing student development.

If a community college seeks to achieve a diverse student population, college leaders must analyze current student demographics. Analysis of recent enrollment and retention trends will highlight the college's successes and gaps in service when contrasted with its potential population base. Comparison of who is attending and who could benefit from the college will help determine future information and recruitment strategies. Understanding how students access college programs and services is another part of the puzzle. Armed with these data, colleges can better communicate to the target markets and develop learning opportunities for potential students throughout the recruitment strategies. The following paragraphs list some market areas and strategies that colleges may find helpful.

K–12 schools. Strengthening the college's relationship with high schools and middle schools in the service area will ensure that K–12 school staff view community colleges as the first enrollment option for students, rather than as a second choice for those unable to immediately enroll in four-year institutions. To achieve this change in attitude, community college leaders can take several steps:

- Hold regular forums with K–12 school officials, including superintendents, principals, and guidance counselors, to discuss how to improve service to them.
- Conduct frequent on-site visits to K–12 schools that include time spent with students and staff.
- Analyze enrollment patterns from area school districts to determine whether the college has greater success in recruiting students from some K–12 districts rather than others, and what contributes to greater success with these districts.
- Develop articulation programs between the high schools and college.
- Work with middle schools to achieve learning success for challenged students.
- Offer college facilities for a school district's staff development day.

College visits and orientations. Colleges need to offer a variety of open house and orientation formats to make it as convenient as possible for students to learn about the institution. Open house and orientation events should also take into consideration different learning and communication styles and practices. To reach diverse learners, colleges must consider whether presentations appeal to and carry the intended messages to different types of students, and whether the advertising for these events appeals appropriately to specific student populations. Successful strategies could include the following:

- Career exploration days where potential students shadow current students or experience "a day in the life of" a community college student and where they can learn from employers about the job and earning potential in specific fields
- Mandatory orientation for new students
- "How-to" days for families regarding financial aid applications, exposure to different careers, or health and fitness

Multicultural resources. Given the demographics of college student populations, offering multicultural student resources is critical. Examples of these resources include the following:

- Tools to identify appropriate communication styles and methods to best share information with communities and students with ESL needs
- Publication of college materials in languages other than English
- Festivals and other cultural events that celebrate holidays important to members of the student body
- Diversity training for staff
- A well-stocked library with up-to-date books, journals, newspapers, and other research sources that reflect students' varied backgrounds and address their interests

It is not enough to have multicultural resources available. In the recruitment phase it is important to *show* prospective students that these resources and experiences are available and to make clear how they can enhance students' learning experiences.

Institutional Example

North Seattle Community College conducted a campus-wide multicultural climate study and systemwide evaluation on the performance of its diverse students. The assessment focused not only on measurements of difference, but also on the changing environments that influence outcomes. Data and anecdotal information were presented to the faculty, resulting in changes made at the course, department, and institutional level. Specifically, the division of social sciences reviewed all curricula and hired a new faculty member specializing in multicultural issues. Training seminars and workshops on multiculturalism were also offered to assist with the redesign and integration of curriculum. (Bers & Mittler, 1994)

Dual enrollment. Dual enrollment is vital to many prospective students. Demonstrating that a college has dual enrollment options with area high schools and universities, and what college services are available to support dual-enrolled students, may make the difference in an individual's choice of one college over another. If there are barriers to increased dual enrollment, such as lack of legislative or funding support, college leaders would be wise to pursue strategies that address the problem.

Learning styles. Prospective students, especially older students, expect college materials—course catalogs, advertisements, learning materials, assisted learning software, and so forth—to appeal to a variety of learning styles, ages, and ethnic backgrounds. In today's high-tech, dynamic, and rapidly changing world, college environments must be both high-tech and high-touch.

ACCESS TO PROGRAMS AND COURSES

Services that help students gain access to programs and activities include registration, enrollment, advising, counseling, assessment, and financial aid. These services are commonly provided by a specific college organizational unit, often referred to as Student Services, Student Development Services, or Student Development and Success. Among student development activities, registration and enrollment probably receive the greatest emphasis because of institutional needs to monitor enrollment for state aid and tuition payments. These units also may include other services available to special student populations, such as veterans, displaced homemakers, students with disabilities, and minority students.

One issue for student development today is how best to integrate changing student needs into existing college structures. This may involve eliminating some structures. Streamlining becomes necessary if bureaucracy-bound colleges are unable to meet the changes in the student body and changes in how they provide educational opportunity.

Leading community colleges use several strategies to promote student access:

- Assign an enrollment adviser or facilitator to each student. Personal contact helps ensure that students learn about program options and requirements while benefiting from the experience and expertise of someone familiar with institutional resources.
- Require assessment testing and course placement before students can enroll.
- Close the gap between high school graduation standards and college admission requirements, and between the community college's graduation requirements and entry requirements of other postsecondary institutions.
- Make tools accessible that help students identify personal characteristics or interests corresponding to particular fields of study.
- Establish internal performance measures to ensure efficient and high-quality registration and enrollment services. For example, adjust expected turnaround times for calculations of financial aid so that aid calculations are consistent with registration and payment deadlines.
- Regularly review processes and systems to identify potential barriers to students in existing procedures. One technique is for the president or staff from other college areas to walk through enrollment and registration. This exercise can reveal, from a student's perspective, strengths and weaknesses in systems and procedures.
- Provide evening and weekend students with the same quality and availability of services that day students receive.
- Provide pertinent college documents (catalogs and course schedules) and support services in languages other than English.
- Incorporate technology into enrollment and registration processes to streamline and simplify the process for students, rather than just using technology to benefit internal operations.

Institutional Example

Sinclair Community College requires all degree/certificate-seeking students to participate in an entry-level assessment and placement process before being allowed to matriculate into regular college courses and access services. SCC students are assessed for reading, language usage and writing, and numerical skills. Students who need to improve these academic skills take developmental education courses to bring their skills up to college-level. Many adult students at the SCC take the Adult Reentry Program in which they are matched with a counselor to discuss their work and educational history, their concerns about learning as an adult student, and their goals while at the college. (Flint & Associates, 1999)

Improving how a college addresses these student access strategies can contribute to enrollment increases. Recruitment and enrollment management are the first steps in student development. The attention leaders pay to services for students once they enter the college is critical if they wish to retain students. A focus on retaining students requires that leaders consider how student development blends with the various learning environments in which students participate.

STUDENT DEVELOPMENT IN THE LEARNING ENVIRONMENT

Student development theory stresses that intellectual growth increases to the extent that students are actively engaged in college learning experiences that include involvement in campus life beyond the classroom. However, community college students frequently must balance work, family, and educational demands that limit their ability to be involved in activities beyond the classroom. This in turn limits growth opportunities.

Community colleges can compensate for limited student involvement by incorporating student development activities into the learning environment, whether that environment is the traditional classroom setting, a course delivered in the workplace, or a distance learning course delivered online. Incorporating student development into all learning environments can promote student success by enhancing the sense of community felt between students whose only common bond may be participating in the same class. This can result in increased student retention rates, an important measure of college success and public accountability.

Community college leaders can use several strategies to ensure that student development concepts are incorporated into the learning environment:

- Link early warning and academic alert systems to academic advising and counseling services. Too often, academic alert systems contact students, who are probably already aware of performance problems, but do not require follow-up with staff who provide specialized services that might improve performance.
- Establish requirements for service and experiential learning opportunities as part of course expectations.
- Plan campus events based on their applicability to course objectives; coordinate special events scheduling with course schedules to ensure that students can attend.
- Ensure that existing and new campus organizations and clubs support college educational programs.

- Encourage faculty to assign internal reviews as class projects. This reduces the need for staff resources and uses student energy and experience to improve the college. Students benefit from valuable experiences that enhance their resumes and job searches. For example, a Madison Area Technical College business technology class conducted a student laptop pilot project. Students evaluated competing laptops, used laptops for courses, and developed a business plan for expanding the pilot program.
- Provide peer-tutoring or mentoring programs to support students as both teachers and learners.
- Conduct periodic surveys of students to identify potential areas of improvement. It may be valuable to contract for survey research tools analyzed by outside consultants. One useful example is the Student Assessment of the College Environment, developed by the National Institute for Leadership and Institutional Effectiveness (n.d.) in Raleigh, North Carolina.
- Offer frequent training opportunities for faculty to enhance their use of assessment tools for identifying where student learning is occurring and where improvements are needed.
- Encourage student services personnel to offer presentations to classes describing the range of services and supports available at the college.

Institutional Example

Maine's York County Technical College (YCTC) developed a College Success Management course to help students learn and adopt strategies that promote their college success. In designing the course, a review of related literature was completed to determine the background and purposes of student success courses, data on student attrition, expected outcomes of the course, and possible course content and formats. Following the review, sample student success course syllabi were obtained from three two-year colleges and a matrix of course content was compiled. Criteria for the course were then developed by a formative committee of one full-time faculty member, one student, one adjunct faculty member, and a dean of students and validated by a summative committee of a high school guidance counselor, the Humanities department chair, and an academic dean. The course covers topics related to library use, dealing with pressures from home, diversity and learning styles, time management, resume development, communication skills, note taking, memory techniques, test-taking strategies, critical thinking, relationships, and health and stress management. (Rainone, 1997)

EXPLORING CAREERS AND FURTHER EDUCATION

Helping students find the right career or educational opportunities is the ultimate test of successful student development. Student development services can play a critical role in helping students to clarify their goals as they prepare to move away from the community college, toward the university, or into a new career. Although this transition process is usually identified with the final semesters of a student's community college experience, exploration of careers and further education can play a significant role in the initial placement of students at the community college. Because students who begin their college careers with a definite goal in mind are more likely to finish school and succeed in their education and on the job, helping newly enrolled students to focus on their future goals in an organized way can result in increased student retention and academic success.

Community college leaders can use several strategies to support student exploration of careers and further education.

Career Exploration

- Require career exploration as part of enrollment and orientation.
- Make online career assessment tools available to all students from both on- and off-campus locations.
- Encourage or require students to review and revise their career or education goals and plans at strategic points throughout their academic careers.
- Link enrollment facilitators, counselors, and advisers with students to interpret results of career assessment and aptitude tests, and to identify programs that relate to student interests and strengths.

Transition to Four-Year Institutions

- Actively pursue articulation agreements with four-year colleges in the area and demonstrate the success of the college's articulation agreements.
- Ensure that enrollment facilitators, counselors, and academic advisers are familiar with admissions requirements for other local colleges and with the steps needed to ensure that credits can be easily and fully transferred.
- Maintain current enrollment and course catalog information for other colleges.
- Regularly invite other colleges to participate in on-campus events and recruiting.

Institutional Example

The City College of San Francisco (CCSF) recognized that issues such as the low rates of transfer among underrepresented groups (especially African American and Hispanic students), financial barriers to transfer due to low socio-economic status, and external factors, such as enforcing Math and English transfer requirements and the rollback of affirmative action, were hindering overall transfer efforts of the college. In response, CCSF formed a Transfer Task Force, which then developed a comprehensive Transfer Enhancement Plan. The purpose of the plan is to improve the transfer success of all CCSF students. The plan is divided into four major areas that explore and enhance CCSF's transfer function: (1) college leadership, (2) academic programs, (3) retention/student support services, and (4) access and outreach. In each of the areas, the goals to be accomplished are highlighted, and strategies and action plans necessary to accomplish each goal are included, as well as associated time frames, resources, and college units responsible for each activity. (CCSF, 1998)

Job searches. Many students, even if they make the transition to a four-year institution, will need to secure employment. By helping them with this transition, the college demonstrates its success as an institution and its value to employers and the public. Employment and spending by graduates creates demonstrable economic impact that helps justify the state and local revenues the colleges may receive. Here are some strategies that colleges may find useful:

- Require internships and externships as part of job preparation.
- Maintain job boards or online employment postings.
- Incorporate nontraditional learning activities into college transcripts to give students a documented competitive edge in the job search process.
- Offer seminars, both off- and online, about job search, application and resume preparation, successful interviewing, and other related topics.
- Track the employment successes of students and report this information in the media, to legislators, and in college recruitment materials.
- Survey employers about their satisfaction with graduates.
- Follow up on employer concerns by implementing improvements in programs and curricula.
- Involve employers in career panels, advisory boards and career fairs.
- Survey alumni about their satisfaction with their training and preparation after they have been employed, and encourage faculty to modify programs and curricula by incorporating feedback and suggestions from graduates.
- Provide career and personnel services online to meet employers' needs for virtual recruiting.

Alumni involvement. Strong alumni relationships may be the best indicator of success in engaging students and making them part of the college community. Low levels of alumni involvement can help show areas of improvements in student development activities. These are some strategies to consider:

- Analyze alumni involvement rates for each college program or department and work to increase involvement in areas with low alumni involvement.
- Regularly survey alumni about how the college could improve the quality of programs, services, and college communities.
- Offer special opportunities to alumni to upgrade their skills.
- Maintain a database or resource list of alumni who may be helpful for specific events or issues.
- Invite alumni to college events or to speak with current students and other stakeholders about their postcollege successes.
- Provide opportunities for classmates to communicate after they leave their programs.
- Thank alumni, both publicly and personally, who provide support through their donations of money, time or other resources.
- Assist alumni with job search needs.

Institutional Example

Oakton Community College (OCC) in Des Plaines, Illinois, utilizes exit interviews and alumni surveys as a form of assessment for programs and services. Like most colleges, they spend significant amounts of time and money producing catalogs, brochures, and other literature in the hope of answering students' questions and informing them about what they need to know to succeed. When they asked students, "Where do you go to find help?"

students indicated that they obtained college information not from the printed materials, but rather from friends, faculty, counselors, and librarians. Basically, they receive most of their information from people. As a result, OCC placed a renewed emphasis on communicating with students by having academic advisers roam registration lines, increasing the availability of faculty advisers, and having identifiable staff available to answer student questions during the start of each quarter. (Bers & Mittler, 1994)

EMERGING ISSUES IN COMMUNITY COLLEGE STUDENT DEVELOPMENT EFFORTS

The changing nature of student populations and the varying workforce skill requirements of employers create more pressure for community colleges to produce well-rounded students who have benefited from personal, emotional, and intellectual growth. Demands for accountability from the public and from elected officials make documented success imperative. With that in mind, college leaders are well advised to review important emerging student development issues, such as the following:

- Conflict mediation between students and between students and faculty
- Campus safety in an age when school and workplace shootings appear to have become almost commonplace
- Remedial education services before students can succeed in meeting educational and career goals
- Demand from students with advanced degrees for community college education and training
- Demand from students with disabilities for community college programs

CONCLUSION

An effective student development environment requires ongoing assessment of how structures, services, and systems must change to meet new demands or to support different student populations. Student development activities may actually be a stimulus for institutional change by affecting the markets and strategies community colleges use to recruit and retain students and employees.

There are no silver bullets when it comes to student development. However, by focusing energy and resources in this critical area, college leaders will move closer to understanding and being able to demonstrate how student support can best be provided. An honest review of a college's current ability to provide the support its students need is the first step in identifying and delivering those services that are truly important to student success.

Recommended Web Sites

Center for Teaching Excellence. Annotated Bibliography of Student Development Literature: http://www.cte.iastate.edu/tips/studdev.html
Central Florida Community College, Resources and Services: http://www.cfcc.cc.fl.us/resources

Douglas College, BC, Canada, Learning Centre:
   http://www.douglas.bc.ca/learning/lchomepg.html
Galveston College, TX, Student Services:
   http://www.gc.edu/stuserv.htm
Germanna Community College, VA, Counseling Services:
   http://www.gc.cc.va.us/counseling
Johnson County Community College, KS, Student Life & Leadership Development:
   http://www.jccc.net/home/depts/001350
J. Sargeant Reynolds Community College, VA, Student Development Services:
   http://www.jsr.cc.va.us/jsr_sds/Default.htm
Kirkwood Community College, IA, Student Development Department:
   http://www.kirkwood.cc.ia.us/studentdev/intro.html
Mayland Community College, NC, Online Catalog:
   http://www.mayland.cc.nc.us/info/pubs/catalog/index.html
National Council on Student Development:
   http://www.nationalcouncilstudentdevelopment.org
Northern Essex Community College, MA, Student Services:
   http://www.necc.mass.edu/student.shtml
Pamlico Community College, North Carolina, Student Development Services:
   http://www.pamlico.cc.nc.us/pcc_student_services.htm
Pellissippi State Technical Community College, TN, Student Resources:
   http://www.pstcc.cc.tn.us/stu.html
Piedmont Technical College, SC, Student Services Division:
   http://www.piedmont.tec.sc.us/student_services/
Richland Community College, IL, Student Development and Services, Study Skills and Learning Assistance:
   http://www.richland.cc.il.us/staff/sblahnik/studyskills.html

References

Bers, T. H., & Mittler, M. L. (Eds.). (1994, Winter). Assessment and testing: Myths and realities. *New Directions for Community Colleges, 88*. (ED391559)

Bourne-Bowie, K. (2000, March). Retention depends on new models of student development. *Black Issues in Higher Education, 17*.

Chickering, A. (1969). *Education and identity*. San Francisco: Jossey-Bass.

City College of San Francisco. (1998). *Transfer enhancement plan: A report prepared by the transfer task force*. Unpublished manuscript. (ED416942)

Flint, T. A., & Associates. (1999). *Best practices in adult learning: A CAEL/APQC benchmarking study*. Chicago: CAEL.

Kuo, E. W. (2000, June). *English as a second language: Program approaches at community colleges*. Los Angeles: ERIC Clearinghouse for Community Colleges. (ED447859)

Mattox, R. E., & Creamer, D. G. (1998). Perceptions of the scope and quality of student services functions in two-year colleges. *Community College Review, 25*.

McCabe, R. H. (2000). *No one to waste: A report to public decision-makers and community college leaders*. Washington, DC: Community College Press.

Merrill, N. (2001). *Learning college principles and student development*. Madison, WI: Madison Area Technical College.

National Institute for Leadership and Institutional Effectiveness. (n.d.). *Student assessment of the college environment*. Survey. Raleigh, NC: Author. (Available from http://www2.ncsu.edu/ncsu/cep/acce/nilie/surveys.html)

O'Banion, T. (1997). *A learning college for the 21st century*. Phoenix: Oryx Press.

Perez, L. X. (1998). Sorting, supporting, connecting and transforming: Intervention strategies for students at risk. *Community College Review, 26*.

Rainone, J. J. (1997). *Development of a college success management course for York County Technical College*. Unpublished manuscript. (ED416916)

Chapter 6

CURRICULUM DEVELOPMENT AND INSTRUCTIONAL DELIVERY

Tony Zeiss

The successful community colleges in the 21st century will be colleges where faculty members can demonstrate that their teaching strategies are in fact causing learning.

—George A. Baker III, from a presentation to the North Carolina Presidents, Lenoir, NC, May 2000

The sweeping changes of the last century have made their impact acutely felt on the curricula and instructional delivery processes at community colleges. All the implications of diversity—ethnicity, gender, age, religious background, economic status, employment status, and marital status—are causing higher education to evolve from a faculty-directed enterprise to a learner-centered one. This does not mean that faculty are becoming irrelevant to the educational experience; rather, their roles are rightfully changing with the times. They are having to become facilitators of learning, rather than playing the traditional role of gatekeepers of knowledge. Likewise, students are expected to participate more actively in the learning experience. In fact, more and more students are demanding involvement in the learning process, and colleges are running in all directions trying to determine the best mix of courses, programs, delivery methods, and support services.

Perhaps the change that has had the greatest effect on curriculum development and instructional delivery is the increase in the number of enrolled adult students. According to the National Center for Education Statistics (NCES), in 2001 approximately 40% of students enrolled in college were 25 or older, with the majority of adult students over the age of 35 (NCES, 2001). This means that, although the majority of students are still the "traditional" 18- to 24-year-olds, the adult student population is larger than previously thought. Furthermore, in 2001, about 40% of college students were enrolled part time—again, a figure higher than most people, educators and the public alike, ever realized (NCES, 2001).

Even more than do younger students, adult students need convenient times and places for learning, because they are typically balancing school with work, home and family life, volunteer or religious activities, and other interests. In general, although not always, adults have a better idea of their educational goals than do younger students, even though they may still need as much or more support from the college in reaching their goals. Other pertinent aspects of having more adult students include the growing importance of workforce training and the provision of access to education and training opportunities through employers (e.g., employer-sponsored training programs or educational benefits such as tuition reimbursement). As well, an influx of immigrants is resulting in a new interest in adult literacy and is placing other, related expectations on community colleges.

College execution strategies addressing curricula and instructional delivery must adapt in specific ways to demonstrate both relevance and value to ever-changing student populations and stakeholder groups. But the execution strategies must also be aligned to those core strategies that a college develops to guide its ongoing strategic activities. In this chapter, I explore some ways to do just that.

COLLEGE LEADERS' ROLES IN CURRICULUM DEVELOPMENT AND INSTRUCTIONAL DELIVERY

Lorenzo and Armes LeCroy (1994) wrote that the time for fundamental change is when society's needs can no longer be met by the institutions that serve it. They accurately suggested that "the overall goal for the community college is to create a culture of responsiveness that more clearly relates its comprehensive mission to these new societal circumstances" (p. 1). Indeed, we must look at the fundamental processes of teaching and learning, curriculum development, and instructional delivery in new ways to ensure that the primary culture of a college—its teaching–learning process—is responsive to a diverse range of students and other college stakeholders. Learners and learning must become the unmistakable priority of the college. Community college leaders must give ample attention to this teaching–learning activity and clearly establish it as a personal leadership priority.

Community colleges have always emphasized teaching and learning as their key mandate and have prided themselves on their accessibility and accountability. Yet in many instances, these champions of teaching and learning have not excelled in measuring their effectiveness or in providing convenient instructional opportunities. Community college leaders may have been diverted from this primary mission while building new facilities and finding the resources to operate them. Other college leaders may have decided that the faculty alone should determine content, instructional methods, and scheduling. In any event, the time has come for community college leaders to become deeply involved in what is taught, how it is taught, and when and where instruction is provided. As O'Banion stated, "Leaders now have a clear mandate to place teaching and learning at the top of the educational agenda in order to repair the neglect of the past and prepare for a new future" (O'Banion, 1994).

This mandate for leaders to become involved in the teaching and learning process does not mean that they alone should determine curriculum, delivery method, or class schedules. Faculty are the rightful developers and keepers of curricula. However, it is incumbent on college leaders to ensure that curricula are based on need, that student-centered instruction is occurring, and that classes are scheduled and delivered in a convenient fashion.

FACULTY ROLES IN CURRICULUM DEVELOPMENT AND INSTRUCTIONAL DELIVERY

Most community college instructors recognize that change is inevitable. They are charged to do more with less; to increase peripheral duties like advising, recruiting, and committee work; and to use new learning technologies to enhance the teaching–learning process. Many seek change, whereas others avoid it altogether. Nevertheless, all faculty will have to develop a new mindset and versatility of skills if they hope to remain effective. The concept that faculty should be "managers of learning" as opposed to "dispensers of knowledge" has really come of age. The instructor for the future must become a renaissance teacher. In the future, instructors will need to be, at the least, information specialists, performers, job placement specialists, advisers, media producers, media performers, mentors, computer whizzes, mediators, budget specialists, TQM experts, collaborators, recruiters, networkers, and learners.

Opportunities to better serve students abound. Community college leaders must find a way to keep the enthusiasm alive and help faculty continue to seize these new opportunities for serving students and their communities in better ways. Teaching and leading in the community college business is a privilege and a dynamic profession indeed!

Institutional Example

Central Piedmont Community College has provided faculty-reviewed "innovation grants" for faculty and staff for more than a decade. These $1,000–$2,000 grants are awarded to employees who want to develop innovative methods for improving student learning. More recently, the board of trustees approved the establishment of a new 501(c)3 organization to provide seed money for innovative and often entrepreneurial activities that enhance the teaching and learning process.

CURRICULUM DEVELOPMENT

According to O'Banion,

> The ideal model of education, the learning college, should inspire substantive change in individual learners, endow them with responsibility for their education, offer as many learning options as possible, assist in collaborative learning activities, define the roles of learning facilitators by the needs of the learners, and record improved and expanded learning. (O'Banion, 1997)

O'Banion summarized the new learning model, in which students take a more active role in learning and faculty become facilitators of learning. Smart college leaders will recognize that the needs of employers must also factor into this new learning model.

Just how well do the curricular offerings at community colleges meet the requirements of this new learning model? The Center for the Study of Community Colleges (CSCC) conducts periodic surveys of the curricula at American community colleges. For the most recent study, in 1998, 164 public community colleges submitted their spring catalogs and schedules. Using student enrollments, the colleges were divided into categories of small (fewer than 2,748), medium (2,749–6,140), and large (more than 6,141). A previously developed coding scheme was applied to track 36 liberal arts and 26 non–liberal arts subjects. The college catalogs and schedules of classes from the sample institutions were coded and tabulated along with enrollment figures. The following is a summary of the results (Striplin, 2000):

Overview

- Fifty-four percent of the course sections in the community college curriculum were in liberal arts.
- As defined by the institutions, 7% of for-credit course sections in the total sample were remedial. The percentages of English and math courses at the remedial level were 29% and 32%, respectively.
- Overall, 74% of liberal arts courses and 34% of non–liberal arts courses were transferable to in-state, four-year public institutions.
- Computer science showed the greatest increase in percentage of enrollment. In the 1991 study, 2% of students were enrolled in computer science. This increased to 4% in the 1998 study.
- The study supported the claim that community colleges offer small class sizes; many academic categories showed small decreases in average class size from 1991 to 1998.
- Although the number of students enrolled in 1998 was comparable to that reported in the prior 1991 study, approximately 30,000 more course sections were offered.

The Liberal Arts

- The humanities, mathematics, science, social science, and fine and performing arts composed the liberal arts.
- In 1998 a higher percentage of colleges offered instruction in each of the 12 disciplines within the humanities.
- Over the years, the sciences have fluctuated in terms of percentage of colleges offering courses and percentage of enrollment. Biology was the most popular science subject, with 100% of the colleges offering at least one course in this field.
- The percentages of English and social science courses offered exhibit considerable stability.
- Between 1991 and 1998 one of the greatest shifts occurred in fine and performing arts, with the percentage of colleges offering these classes increasing dramatically.

Non–Liberal Arts Curriculum

- Results from both the 1991 and 1998 surveys indicated that the non–liberal arts curriculum accounted for less than 50% of the total community college curriculum.
- In colleges where a high proportion of liberal arts courses were accepted by universities, a similarly high proportion of non–liberal arts courses were accepted.
- In 1998 at least 90% of the community colleges offered classes in business and office skills, marketing and distribution, health sciences, computer applications, and education.

General Education Requirements

- A statement of the objectives of general education was included in more than half of the colleges' catalogs.
- Distribution requirements, the dominant forms of general education requirements, were part of the largest proportion of academic degree programs (69%) and a significant proportion of occupational degree programs (29%).

- Acquiring basic academic skills, especially composition and mathematics, was highly represented in statements of general education objectives for both academic and occupational degrees.
- Seventy-six percent of the schools required some computer literacy course in the transfer degree programs, whereas 86% required it for the nontransfer degree programs.

Interdisciplinary Studies

- Overall, interdisciplinary courses constituted 1% of the total community college curriculum and just under 2% of the liberal arts curriculum.
- More than half of the colleges offered some type of interdisciplinary course in the sciences, ranging from 1 to 20 sections.
- Fifty-six interdisciplinary courses were offered as distance education courses, using television, the Internet, and video as modes of delivery.
- From 1991 to 1998, the average number of interdisciplinary courses offered per institution increased from four to five.

Honors Programs

- Thirty-six percent of the institutions studied offered honors programs to their students.
- Colleges with either larger enrollments or a higher proportion of transfer courses were more likely to offer honors courses.
- A negative relationship was found between the proportion of some minority groups and the availability of an honors program.

English as a Second Language

- A 15% increase in ESL course offerings was found, indicating that ESL programs still constitute a growing element of the community college curriculum.
- Institutional size played an important role in ESL course availability. Of the large community colleges, more than half offered more than 20 ESL courses.
- Geographic location of the institution also influenced the number of ESL courses offered: the West, Midwest, and the Middle Atlantic states accounted for 71% of the ESL curriculum.
- At two colleges, each of which reported having a large ESL program, ESL courses made up more than 14% of all available courses.

Multicultural Education

- In 1998 the percentage of colleges offering ethnic studies rose to 26% following a decline from 1975 (15%) to 1991 (9%).
- The ways in which multicultural courses meet the general education requirements varied from institution to institution.
- Overall, the number of courses offered and the number of students enrolled in multicultural courses were relatively small.

Distance Education

- One hundred twenty-eight colleges (78%) offered at least one distance education course. The number of courses ranged from 1 to 67, with an average of 20 distance education classes per institution.
- Only 2% of the 139,083 courses were offered through distance education.
- There was a direct relationship between the total number of distance education courses and college enrollment.
- The highest percentage of distance education classes was in the social sciences and the lowest percentage in biological sciences and foreign languages. (Striplin, 2000)

The results of this study provide only a snapshot of the state of the national community college curriculum; measuring the true level of change in curriculum development will require more and different types of research. However, a few conclusions may be drawn from the CSCC study:

- Community colleges offer unique courses, but many curricular trends span institutional boundaries.
- The number of students enrolled at community colleges is increasing dramatically, and colleges are diversifying the types of courses and programs they offer to their students.
- Although ESL, distance education, computer instruction, and business-related courses have increased somewhat, the traditional liberal arts curriculum remains relatively stable and dominant in community college offerings.

To move in the direction O'Banion and others suggest, curricula must be developed through a collaborative process involving faculty teams and other content experts, especially those who will employ the college's graduates. Students can no longer be expected to conform to instructor-driven schedules or accept archaic curricula. Successful colleges and faculty will view themselves as customer-focused and as part of a larger community. Basic academic curricula, for example, should include opportunities for learning global competence and world affairs in a contextual manner. The Internet has provided real-time, global experiences for all learners, and it should be used as a basic tool for interactive learning. All career-based curricula should cover the basic workplace skills, including communication, work ethic, teamwork, analytical skills, and the importance of a positive attitude. In effect, faculty and all writers of curricula should become holistic in their thinking, contextual in their writing, and learning-focused in their teaching.

Dolence (2000) pointed out the need to establish a framework for the development of learner and learning-centered curricula. His framework requires curriculum architects to place their curricula in a 21st-century context that focuses on the learner. He suggested that curriculum developers should ask themselves the following five questions to try to shape curricula from the learner's perspective:

1. When you want to learn something, *when* do you want to learn it?
2. When you want to learn something, *why* do you want to learn it?
3. When you want to learn something, *what* do you want to learn?
4. When you want to learn something, *how* do you want to learn it?
5. When you want to learn something, *where* do you want to learn it?

Even better, ask the students directly. Baker surveyed 10,000 community college students in 1998 and asked them two salient questions: Why do you attend community colleges? And, for those who began but did not complete their studies at a community college, why did you leave? The majority said that they enrolled to gain occupational skills, for financial reasons, or because of inconvenient class scheduling. These responses reinforce the urgent need for colleges to develop a curriculum that is convenient, offers a better mix of occupational skills and traditional liberal arts knowledge, and is bolstered by increased financial aid opportunities, such as grants and scholarships for part-time students.

Some new models for curricula are emerging. For example, the Council for Adult and Experiential Learning (CAEL) suggested creating a broad curriculum while also developing a focused set of individualized learning goals (cited in Flint & Associates, 1999). In its landmark 1999 benchmarking study of institutions that excel at serving adult learners, CAEL outlined some core components that would strengthen curriculum at higher education institutions. According to CAEL, a well-designed curriculum should meet the following criteria:

- Be designed to meet the individual needs of a diverse population of adult and traditional learners
- Include fixed and flexible components that help learners clearly identify their individual learning needs and goals
- Incorporate both informal and formal assessment procedures
- Allow for identification and evaluation of prior learning
- Allow for the development of individualized learning plans that enable learners to track their progress in completing the curriculum
- Include options that allow it to be easily adapted for each individual student or for groups of students with common learning needs and goals

In the ever-evolving area of distance education, the Higher Learning Commission (HLC) of the North Central Association, one of the regional accrediting agencies in the United States, has articulated a definition of distance education and guidelines for institutions to follow in preparing to meet the requirements of accreditation. The definition and the guidelines for distance learning curriculum development are as follows:

> Distance education is defined, for the purposes of accreditation review, as a formal educational process in which the majority of the instruction occurs when student and instructor are not in the same place. Instruction may be synchronous or asynchronous. Distance education may employ correspondence study, or audio, video, or computer technologies.

Guidelines: Any institution offering distance education is expected to meet the requirements of its own regional accrediting body, and be guided by the Western Interstate Commission for Higher Education (WICHE) Principles. In addition, an institution is expected to address, in its self-studies and/or proposals for institutional change, the following expectations, which it can anticipate will be reviewed by its regional accrediting commission.

Curriculum and Instruction

- Programs provide for timely and appropriate interaction between students and faculty, and among students.
- The institution's faculty assumes responsibility for and exercises oversight over distance education, ensuring both the rigor of programs and the quality of instruction.
- The institution ensures that the technology used is appropriate to the nature and objectives of the programs.
- The institution ensures the currency of materials, programs, and courses.
- The institution's distance education policies are clear concerning ownership of materials, faculty compensation, copyright issues, and the utilization of revenue derived from the creation and production of software, telecourses, or other media products.
- The institution provides appropriate faculty support services specifically related to distance education.
- The institution provides appropriate training for faculty who teach in distance education programs. (HLC, 2002)

The HLC has also recently proposed new criteria for accreditation of its member institutions. The new criteria are intended to better reflect the priorities and challenges facing two- and four-year colleges and universities at the beginning of the 21st century. The proposed changes that would relate to how community colleges develop curricula are included in two criteria:

Criterion Three: Student Learning and Effective Teaching

Evidence about curricular currency and relevance:

- Regular program reviews include attention to currency and relevance of programs and courses.
- Learning outcomes reflect expected workplace competencies.
- Curricular evaluation involves alumni, employers, and other external constituents who understand the relationship between the course of study, the currency of the curriculum, and the utility of the knowledge and skills gained.
- Faculty actively participate in professional organizations relevant to their teaching disciplines.

Criterion Four: Discovery

Evidence about program and curricular innovations that support discovery:

- Multiple opportunities exist for applied practice.
- Resources support student development and co-curricular activities.
- Internal and external support exists for research, partnerships, innovations, and new programs. (HLC, 2002)

The guidelines provided by CAEL and the HLC reflect a maturing grasp of the issues related not only to curriculum development, but also to all aspects of how colleges serve learners, from mission to operations. Currency and relevance are common themes that are driving colleges all across the country to reevaluate and revise the effectiveness of their curricula.

Institutional Example

Sinclair Community College primarily offers traditional, pre-designed vocational and academic transfer associate degrees and certificates . . . [However,] within these degrees and certificates, curriculum is developed primarily in response to local economic development efforts. Skill mismatches between companies and the workforce have been identified as a local problem, and many companies have begun to develop competencies for entry-level positions. The College profiles students to determine gaps between their competencies and the ones needed by the companies, and then students take course modules to fill the gaps. . . .

Beyond the core courses, students can choose to tailor a degree to their individual goals through the assistance of the Experienced Based Education staff and departmental faculty. The Associate of Individualized Study degree is open to any student who wishes to design an interdisciplinary degree program in the liberal arts or combining liberal arts with technical areas of study. Alternatively, the Associate of Technical Study degree is open to any student whose technical degree goals cannot be accomplished through enrollment in one of Sinclair's existing degree programs. These tailored degrees often incorporate more in-depth prior learning assessment than other degrees at the college. A degree planning seminar provides guidance in the planning of these individualized degrees and a capstone course focuses on reflective learning and documentation of mastery in subject areas studied at the point of program completion.

One of Sinclair Community College's core indicators of instructional effectiveness is "Community Focus" and this is manifested in numerous partnerships with business and industry that result in specialized curriculum. The AIM (Advanced Integrated Manufacturing) Center has an economic development goal to make Dayton [Ohio] companies more competitive. AIM focuses on helping companies solve critical path problems, assessing training needs in relation to these problems, and providing a customized course offering to fill the training need. About 40–50 companies a year participate in these partnerships with the college, and such partnerships last between two and four years. . . .

All vocational degrees at [Sinclair] have documented learning competencies, and degrees come with a money-back guarantee that graduates can demonstrate those competencies. The competencies were established with the assistance of advisory committees, professional bodies, and employers. An example of a college partnership with the community that influences the curriculum is: the chairperson of Sinclair's Management division sits on the Board of Directors of Iams Co., and someone from that organization is on the Management division's advisory board. Courses in vocational programs are tightly tied to industry standards. (Flint & Associates, 1999)

The experience of Sinclair Community College illustrates one strategy—a modularized approach to curriculum—that many colleges are beginning to experiment with to meet the needs of constituencies and to satisfy new standards for accreditation and accountability. With the mandate to serve multiple populations in a variety of ways, the need to modularize both credit and noncredit curricula is essential. Establishing a skills-stacking, or certificate-stacking structure, which equates academic as well as technical skills to traditional credentials including degrees, makes sense for students and for the college. However, it is no longer important that all skills training be provided in the form of college credit. Indeed, fewer students now complete technical degrees. They simply wish to acquire the skills necessary to get work and to progress in their careers. A competency-based, modularized curriculum paves the way for multiple delivery in credit or noncredit settings. This curriculum structure will allow students to easily develop lifetime résumés of their skills and credentials, will help employers assess applicant consistency and employee needs, and will help colleges be more responsive.

Colleges will be required to update curricula to factor in the needs of learners, employers, and communities, but this does not mean they should abandon the principles and values upon which all curricula are based. All curricula, academic or skills-oriented, must adhere to the principles of civic responsibility and respect for others. Certainly, colleges must reform to meet emerging needs with process and content adjustments, but the ethics of teaching and the integrity of the curriculum should remain. This is an exciting time. It is a time to enthusiastically embrace and continue the traditions of access and responsiveness.

NEW DELIVERY ALTERNATIVES

Community college students have jobs, families, and a host of demands for their time, and they are less patient with instruction and instructional methods that do not provide immediate benefit. Therefore, providing convenient access to learning is critical. Although the traditional lock-step, lecture method will surely remain as an alternative delivery style, more convenient, collaborative, and contextual methods for learning—better suited for today's learners—are appearing and will continue to be developed in the future. Panitz (1999) has said that collaborative learning, which promotes human interactions through cooperation, is the favored educational paradigm and that learning as a team promotes social support systems and increased individual achievement (1999). Dinchak (1999) described the learner-centered classroom and its benefits, listing six key elements of the learning classroom:

1. The learning classroom creates substantive change in learners.
2. The learning classroom engages learners as full partners in learning.
3. The learning classroom creates and offers as many learning options as possible.
4. The learning classroom helps learners to participate in collaborative activities.
5. The learning classroom defines the roles of learning facilitators by the needs of the learners.
6. The learning classroom and its learning facilitators succeed only when improved and expanded learning is documented.

Talking about collaborative learning and optional learning methods is easy. Preparing faculty and an instructional landscape to deliver learning-centered instruction is another matter. Some faculty members are reluctant to change. Sometimes they believe they will lose control of the class if it is not tightly structured. Even students who have learned via the seat-time and lecture method all their lives frequently resist group learning and individual learning options.

Felder and Brent (1996) discussed these issues in a very practical manner. They argued that the benefits of student-centered instruction (SCI) are indeed tangible and not only immediate. They encourage faculty and students alike to be patient with the process, acknowledging many of the concerns faculty have about SCI, such as these:

- "If I spend time in class on active learning exercises, I'll never get through the syllabus."
- "If I don't lecture I'll lose control of the class."
- "I assign readings but many of my students don't read them and those who do seem unable to understand the material independently."
- "Some of my students just don't seem to get what I'm asking them to do—they keep trying to find 'the right answer' to open-ended problems, they still don't have a clue about what a critical question is, and the problems they make up are consistently trivial."
- "I'm having a particularly hard time getting my students to work in teams. Many of them resent having to do it and a couple of them protested to my department head about it."
- "Teams working together on quantitative problem assignments may always rely on one or two members to get the problem solutions started. The others may then have difficulties on individual tests, when they must begin the solutions themselves."
- "I teach a class containing students in minority populations that tend to be at risk academically. Does active, cooperative learning work in this kind of setting?"

Fortunately, the present time allows for myriad instructional alternatives, whether delivered in a student-centered, action-learning, or lecture-based course. "Smart classrooms," with every type of audio and video equipment imaginable, are becoming commonplace on community college campuses. These classrooms often provide interactive video and Internet connections. Telecourses and Internet courses have become viable alternatives for students with schedule or work conflicts, and multiple in-class delivery activities have become popular.

The secret to delivering content in a variety of ways is to deliver it in a modularized fashion. Curricula can be delivered in multiple ways if material is organized by sequential competencies. Open computer labs, technology-enhanced libraries, and learning centers are providing meaningful support for distance learning students, as well as for campus-bound students. Student services administrators are beginning to recognize that support services should be provided to evening and nontraditional students at the same level of quality and availability as for daytime, traditional students.

Institutional Example

The theme of Sinclair Community College's array of instructional delivery strategies is that learning can be any time, any way, and any where. Instructional delivery options from which students can choose are:

- Group courses at times convenient to all three work shifts, including midnight to 7:00 A.M. with faculty office hours at 3:00 A.M.
- TV Sinclair courses, offered in three formats—videocassette lectures, audiocassette lectures, and written lectures (print-based). Seventy courses enroll more than 2,500 students.
- Sinclair Electronic College courses, made available on the Internet and World Wide Web. Students may access course information and assignments, ask questions and pose discussion topics, or link to other databases and resources on the Web.

- Courses offered in 14 geographic locations.
- Two degrees offered completely through distance education.
- Through a consortium of League for Innovation colleges, more than 500 credit courses and numerous non-credit courses are offered through distance education.
- Non-classroom, individualized learning contracts are offered through the College Without Walls program (more than 1,000 students involved per year).
- Through a regional television network, interactive voice, video, and data communication is provided on four channels. Courses are offered live to off-campus sites equipped with special receiver antennas, classroom monitors, and telephones. Sites include area high schools, an air force base, businesses, career centers, and other locations.
- Accelerated and integrated block courses are offered in a combination of evening, Saturday, and distance education formats to enable students to efficiently earn their transfer degrees.

To support Sinclair faculty in their exploration of new instructional delivery modes, the College maintains a 76,000 sq. ft. Center for Interactive Learning. The Center serves as a laboratory in which Sinclair faculty can conduct application research and develop interactive learning methods, including the use of electronic information resources and instructional technologies. (Flint & Associates, 1999)

CONCLUSION

Professional development for community college employees, especially faculty, is paramount to ensuring the future success of community colleges. Yet preparing faculty to deliver new and expanded services in a variety of alternative ways has become a major challenge for community college leaders. Many colleges do provide faculty development opportunities, but few require a mandatory number of training hours per year, and fewer still require any specified training. If training in new delivery methods is not provided, how can a leader expect a change in curriculum or instructional delivery? Fortunately, there is reason for optimism. Community college leaders are aware of the need to become more customer-focused and community-based. If community college leaders and their faculty remain steadfast in the founding values of access and responsiveness, they will continue to lead the way in higher education.

References

Baker, G. A., III (1998, April/May). Keeping all generations happy: The Xers, boomers, and beyond... *The Community College Journal,* p.10.

Dinchak, M. (1999, May). *Using the World Wide Web to create a learner-centered classroom.* Los Angeles: ERIC Clearinghouse for Community Colleges. (ED433047)

Dolence, M. G., & Associates. (2000). A primer on building a learner centered curriculum. Available from www.mgdolence.com

Felder, R. M., & Brent, R. (1996). Navigating the bumpy road to student-centered instruction. *College Teaching, 44*(2), 43–47. Retrieved from http://www2.ncsu.edu/unity/lockers/users/f/felder/public/Papers/Resist.html

Flint, T. A., & Associates. (1999). *Best practices in adult learning: A CAEL/APQC bench-marking study*. Chicago: Council for Adult and Experiential Learning.

Higher Learning Commission. (2002). *Proposed new criteria for accreditation*. Retrieved from http://www.hlcommission.org/resources/Criteria_Indicators.pdf

Lorenzo A. L., & Armes LeCroy, N. (1994). *A framework for fundamental change in the community college: Creating a culture of responsiveness*. Macomb, MI: Macomb Community College Press.

National Center for Education Statistics. (2001). *Projections of education statistics to 2011*. Retrieved from http://nces.ed.gov/pubs2001/proj01/tables/table14.asp

O'Banion, T. (1994). Teaching and learning: A mandate for the nineties. *The Community College Journal, 64*(4), 20–25.

O'Banion, T. (1997). *Creating more learning-centered community colleges*. Mission Viejo, CA: League for Innovation in the Community College. (ED414980)

Panitz, T. (1999, December). *The case for student centered instruction via collaborative learning paradigms*. Los Angeles: ERIC Clearinghouse for Community Colleges. (ED448444)

Striplin, J. C. (2000, February). *A review of community college curriculum trends*. Los Angeles: ERIC Clearinghouse for Community Colleges. (ED438011)

Chapter 7

COMMUNITY, ECONOMIC, AND WORKFORCE DEVELOPMENT

Tony Zeiss

Leadership should be born out of the understanding of the needs of those who would be affected by it.

—Marian Anderson

It is widely acknowledged today that education and prosperity are inextricably linked for individuals, organizations, businesses, and communities. The need for effective education at all levels has never been greater, and equipping people with the knowledge and skills to be productive is what community colleges must be about. Citizens, policymakers, and business leaders across the nation now recognize the value and importance of community colleges; colleges have unprecedented opportunities to demonstrate relevance and to fulfill the mission of serving communities in more significant ways.

It will take informed and sometimes courageous community college leaders to maintain institutional relevance in this new century. Convincing faculty and other stakeholders of the necessity to play an expanded role connecting to the world beyond the college campus—particularly through community, economic, and workforce development initiatives—is already presenting a challenge for community college leaders. Nonetheless, it is imperative that community colleges listen and respond to the needs of the people, businesses, and communities they serve. Community colleges must continue to embrace their core value of accessibility by becoming accessible in new and more meaningful ways.

How colleges connect to the broader community, how they act as leaders shaping the futures of the broader community, and how they reflect those connections and future visions in their core strategies and translate them into specific operational or execution strategies—these issues are at the heart of what it means to lead transformational change at a community college. In this chapter I describe ways in which community college leaders can craft effective community, workforce, and economic development strategies that fit within an overarching strategic framework and are aligned with the long-term mission and vision statements of their institutions.

EFFECTIVE LEADERSHIP STRATEGIES FOR COMMUNITY, ECONOMIC, AND WORKFORCE DEVELOPMENT

Community development can be defined in many ways, depending on the goals and objectives of the community partners that are doing the "developing." For example, some view community development simply as a more intensive, more comprehensive approach to economic development. Others use the phrase "sustainable community development" to emphasize not only the economic aspects but also the long-term land and resource use, environmental, and health issues facing many communities. One common thread that seems to run through all definitions is that community development involves citizens, organizations, and other stakeholders engaging in ongoing dialogue to identify priority issues and to create action plans for addressing them. In a sense, then, community development is really strategic planning and implementation at a community-wide level.

Economic development and workforce development are integral parts of community development. In this regard, *economic development* can be defined as those activities that result in the attraction and retention of employers, and hence the creation or retention of jobs, which contribute to a community's prosperity. National trends in economic development indicate that state or regional strategies focusing on specific industries or business sectors are proving to be most effective. *Workforce development*, from the community college perspective, can be defined as those learning activities that prepare workers for jobs, promotions, or career advancement and that assist employers with articulating and meeting their skill needs. There is also a larger workforce development picture in which community colleges are one of numerous partners coordinating strategies and resources for the benefit of an entire region.

The fundamental role of community colleges in this landscape is primarily to prepare people for work and citizenship. From basic skills to English as a second language (ESL), to transfer degrees, skill certifications, and customized curricula for employers, unions, and industry groups, community colleges have become major players in community, economic, and workforce development around the country. A 1997 landmark study designed to produce a blueprint for building strong economies featured the exemplary workforce development activities of America's community colleges (Zeiss, 1997). Community colleges have clearly become the economic engines of their communities.

Ideally, college leadership strategies with regard to community, economic, and workforce development activities should not be created in a vacuum but should grow out of deep connections between the college and other community stakeholders. If they are not already doing so, college presidents and members of their executive teams should be actively participating in or helping to launch regional collaborative efforts in community development. Regardless of the level of involvement of an institution in these types of initiatives, there are some general strategies that may prove useful as a starting point. These and more specific community, economic, and workforce development strategies are described as follows.

- Be certain that your college's vision and mission are relevant to current and anticipated community needs.
- Understand and embrace your college's vision, mission, and values.
- Be certain your trustees embrace your college's vision, mission, and values.
- Get your faculty and staff to support the vision, mission, and values.
- Communicate the college's vision, mission, and values to the community.
- Conduct continuous environmental scans of your internal and external community needs, emphasizing the needs of your multiple populations.
- Continuously monitor and evaluate how your college is meeting community and learner needs.

- Treat your employees as professionals and as your greatest assets.
- Anticipate change and help your employees anticipate change.
- Expect the best from your employees.
- Share the glory, accept the blame.
- Learn to think strategically and from multiple dimensions, political, social, ethical, and financial.
- Protect the college's image at all costs.
- Become a transformational leader, tying change to core values of the college.
- Recognize that your authority is earned on a daily basis, not granted.
- Lead with humility, integrity, kindness, and enthusiasm.
- Learn to sell ideas and your college well.

Institutional Example

The Michigan Environmental Scanning Consortium is a consortium of Michigan community colleges, workforce investment boards, and other workforce development organizations. MSCAN exists to enable consortium members to collect, access, and analyze information, tools, and resources relevant to the environmental scanning process. Its secondary purpose is to support the coordination and strategic planning of workforce development system programs and services through good data collection and analysis. Having community colleges as members of the consortium confirms the importance of the role the colleges play in workforce development efforts in the state of Michigan. Twenty-six Michigan community colleges participate in MSCAN and related activities.

COMMUNITY DEVELOPMENT STRATEGIES

Community colleges can connect to community development efforts by engaging in dialogue with key stakeholders:

- County and municipal planning agencies
- Downtown development authorities
- Community development corporations (CDCs)
- Community action boards
- Community-based organizations, such as neighborhood associations, nonprofit service organizations, and faith-based charities
- K–12 educators
- Health care facilities
- Transportation agencies
- Utility companies

Community colleges can bring many assets to community development partnerships, from delivering education and training services that support the achievement of community-wide goals to playing a leadership role in setting standards for the education of a community's citizens. Each college must determine the community services it should and can provide, based on its unique time, place, and fiscal circumstances. These are some of the relevant offerings at community colleges today: adult and family literacy education; ESL programs; international education; neighborhood leadership training; convenient delivery of services; cultural activities; youth support programs (such as Trio programs); forums for community relations, workforce development; and so forth.

Institutional Example

The Building College and Community Services for Single Parents and Displaced Homemakers Project at Austin Community College, Texas, achieved its goals for successive years. In Project Year 1994–1995 (the most recent data available), the project accomplished the following:

- Developed cooperative linkages with 12 businesses and community organizations
- Actively recruited more than 1,200 displaced homemakers and single parents, with 212 enrolling in vocational and technical education
- Effectively retained disadvantaged students through training and support services
- Assisted in the school-to-work transition of graduating project participants
- Provided support services to 586 enrolled students who were single parents and displaced homemakers, with 90 of them receiving financial assistance to defray the cost of dependent care or textbooks and supplies
- Saw the 82 students who received financial assistance from the project during fall and spring semesters maintain an average earned grade point average of 3.1 and retained 89% of students through spring or summer
- Provided assistance to 381 single-parent prospective students through career and educational planning or resource information
- Helped students gain access to alternative means of financial and other types of aid (adapted from Texas Higher Education Coordinating Board, 1995)

In addition to providing services, community colleges often take leadership positions with regard to education, training, and workforce development. One strategy that has proven particularly effective for community colleges is community-based programming (CBP). CBP is defined as

> a cooperative process that involves a series of tasks in which the community college serves as the leader and catalyst in effecting collaboration among the people, their leaders, and other community-based organizations and agencies within its service area in identifying and seeking resolution to major issues that are of critical concern to the community and its people. (Boone, 1992, cited in Holub, 1996)

CBP is used by community colleges as a way to become familiar with and responsive to the problems facing their varying constituencies.

There is some evidence that CBP is perceived as easier to implement in urban and metropolitan areas than in rural areas, because of the abundance and proximity of stakeholder groups in metropolitan areas. As Gillett-Karam stated, "the rural United States is known by a set of identifiers that include the words low, slow and high-low population density, low total populations, low per-capita income, low levels of educational attainment, slow job growth, high poverty, high unemployment, and high rates of illiteracy" (1995, cited in Holub, 1996). Gillett-Karam emphasized that these conditions persist and are exacerbated by the rapid and overwhelming changes in the national and global economy. The movement from a rural, agrarian society to an urban industrial society was completed long ago. Today, there is the additional burden of surviving in the newly emerging market system, a system that has catapulted society into a global arena, not only for corporate entities, but for the general population as well. The combination of these factors has served to further isolate rural communities from the benefits they might receive if they had greater access to what the current economic trends have to offer. College leaders in rural areas may find it well worth their while to make the extra effort of using a CBP approach to program design and delivery.

Institutional Example

Among the more successful programs using the CBP approach is Project ACCLAIM (Academy for Community College Leadership Advancement, Innovation and Modeling), which is operated by North Carolina State University. James Sprunt Community College, a rural institution in North Carolina that participated in Project ACCLAIM, assisted the Appalachian Regional Steering Committee with developing the following strategies designed to help community colleges address the issue of rural illiteracy:

Policy Strategies

- Identify and work with community opinion leaders and obtain a commitment from those leaders to work together to identify educational deficiencies of the rural adult.
- Prepare leaders to train others to become involved in community development activities.
- Form community coalitions who will influence legislators as well as identify and obtain outside resources.
- Utilize every possible means to obtain visibility for the area.

Dispositional Strategies

- Conduct a public relations campaign promoting equal opportunity for rural adults.
- Encourage institutions to establish peer support groups, provide career planning activities, establish orientation programs, and develop nonpunitive grading systems.

Situational Strategies

- Lobby for legislation to allow deductions for the costs of transportation and child care so as not to penalize those on public assistance.
- Form cooperative agreements with public schools for joint use of buses or establish college transportation systems.
- Lobby for reduced student-paid costs for public postsecondary education and to improve the present student-aid system.

Institutional Strategies

- Identify and publicize model cooperative partnerships.
- Develop cooperative partnership agreements between and among agencies at all levels.
- Establish a tie between institutional accountability for cooperation and institutional funding.
- Provide incentives to individual faculty and to institutions to encourage their serving rural students.
- Capitalize on existing technology such as satellite systems and cable television to provide access to rural areas (adapted from Holub, 1996)

ECONOMIC DEVELOPMENT STRATEGIES

Community colleges can connect to economic development efforts by engaging in dialogue with key stakeholders, such as the following:

- Local, regional, and state economic development agencies
- County and municipal planning agencies
- State and regional economic development organizations
- Employers
- Employer groups, such as chambers of commerce, small business development associations, and industry associations
- Labor unions
- Other community or technical colleges in the region
- University economic and political science departments
- CDCs
- Community-based organizations, such as neighborhood associations, nonprofit service organizations, and faith-based charities

Assets that community colleges bring to economic development partnerships include the range of programs and services that support business development, from the growing number of community college business and industry centers to employee training for new or relocating companies, to certificates of entrepreneurship for individuals who want to launch their own businesses. Here are some examples of economic development activities at community colleges today:

- Helping entrepreneurs start businesses
- Providing import–export training
- Providing public–private procurement services
- Assisting small businesses with needs identification and service referrals
- Providing general business, sales, and marketing training
- Providing business-related research support
- Establishing a user-friendly Web page for entrepreneurs
- Developing a business incubator program and facility

WORKFORCE DEVELOPMENT STRATEGIES

Workforce development is really the core role of community colleges in the larger community and economic development landscape. Almost everything community colleges do is related to workforce development. With the exception of avocational courses, the entire curriculum focuses on the teaching and learning of career-related knowledge and skills. Although personal enrichment is still a strong reason why people enroll at community colleges, a growing number of students in the arts, humanities, sciences, professions, and technologies are seeking the knowledge and skills to help them with their careers, with an emphasis on careers and jobs that pay well and will lead to prosperity for individuals and communities.

Fortunately, no educational system is better positioned than community colleges to help propel their communities into a healthy and prosperous future. Workforce development offerings at community colleges today include the following:

Customized Assessment

- Validated occupational analysis of needed skills
- Customized screenings and evaluations
- Basic skills evaluations
- Industry-specific basic skills assessments

Customized Training

- Job analysis profiling
- Curriculum development
- Instructional analysis for best delivery
- Customized and convenient training, both off- and on-site

Employee Retention Initiatives

- Customized assessment and screening
- Industry-specific research
- Employee recognition strategies
- Management and supervisory analysis and training

Support Services

- Credit and noncredit skills training
- Business information center
- New program and certification development
- Certification development (customized technical degrees)
- Labor–management mediation
- State economic job training grant acquisition and implementation

Job Recruitment Activities

- Working closely with local economic development organizations
- Serving on recruitment teams
- Developing a regional economic workforce development partnership with high schools, other community colleges, universities, employers, and other stakeholders
- Showcasing college capabilities at area organizations and events
- Serving on relevant boards and commissions
- Consulting with prospective new companies on workforce needs
- Writing legislation to support free training for new and existing businesses

Institutional Example

In Michigan, economic and workforce development increasingly leans toward the integration of the two areas. The Michigan Economic Development Corporation (MEDC), the state-level economic development agency, actively promotes workforce initiatives as part of its economic development agenda. The MEDC also works closely with the state's community college system, through the Michigan Community College Association, and includes community colleges as a keystone of statewide economic and workforce development success. In a 2002 white paper, the MEDC listed its recommendations for improving the state's workforce development system, which included the following:

1. Develop a unified marketing strategy, directed toward students and their parents. The MEDC should gather stakeholders, including the Michigan Works! Agencies, Michigan Community College Association, and the Michigan Department of Career Development (MDCD), to develop a strategic plan for improving the coordination and marketing of technical careers being created in the new economy. The plan needs to address the following:

   - The need for more technical education at both the community college and university levels
   - New ways to describe "technical education" given the negative perception of vocational training programs
   - More creative thinking about how to pursue a technically oriented career (2+2 programs, as an example)
   - The issue of students making career choices based on their perceptions rather than on actual labor market conditions
   - The perception of parents and students that the student should possess a high level of employability skills
   - The perception that a traditional four-year general education degree is more valuable than technical careers

2. Review and better align financial incentives and policies, including shifting current resources, to ensure that scholarships, grants, and loans fully support the training needs of technical careers.
3. Build a skill-based credentialing system to ensure quality and consistency to customers currently being served in the community college system. The Michigan Community

College Association should develop, in coordination with the MDCD and MEDC and based on the input from private and public sector representatives, a model for a credentialing system recognized statewide that addresses the needs of its customers (employers and students). (adapted from MEDC, 2002)

CONCLUSION

Being responsive to communities is and always has been a core mission of community and technical colleges. In large measure, the value and accountability of community colleges are determined by how well they position themselves to be at the forefront of community, economic, and workforce initiatives. Indeed, the economic health of communities is now largely determined by the responsiveness of community colleges and other educational institutions. A crucial element is the capacity of college leaders to recommit their colleges to their communities; embrace community, economic, and workforce development; be transformational leaders; and think and act strategically.

References

Holub, J. D. (1996, January). The role of the rural community college in rural community development. Los Angeles: ERIC Clearing House for Community Colleges. (ED391558)

Michigan Economic Development Corporation. (2002). *Workforce and career development: Building upon key Michigan strengths.* Retrieved from http://www.mcca.org/MEDCWhitePaper.pdf

Texas Higher Education Coordinating Board. (1995). *Building college and community services for single parents and displaced homemakers: PY95 final detailed report.* Austin: Author. (ED395167)

Zeiss, T. (Ed.). (1997). *Developing the world's best workforce: An agenda for America's community colleges.* Washington, DC: Community College Press.

Chapter 8

STAFF DEVELOPMENT

Beverly Simone

The ultimate leader is one who is willing to develop people to the point that they eventually surpass him or her in knowledge and ability.

—Fred A. Manske, Jr. (1999)

Good staff development, like all of the strategic areas discussed in this book, can be challenging for several reasons. First, the rate of change in technology and science, and the explosion of knowledge in nearly all academic disciplines, mandates ongoing learning by college employees. This is critical to a college's ability to maintain quality degree and certification programs and support services. Second, the wide range of staff positions at community colleges requires that college leaders identify training and development issues common to all staff, as well as provide training opportunities that address specific training needs of individuals, departments, or cross-functional teams. Third, staff development has traditionally emphasized top-level managers and faculty. In today's community college environment, all college employees must be assured of adequate opportunities to enhance their personal and professional development. Training and development for new hires and existing staff must be among the priorities in order to retain workers and enhance job performance. College leaders must also consider development needs from different perspectives: those of support staff, faculty, mid-level managers, and the leaders themselves, including both college presidents and trustees.

How college leaders approach staff development is integral to their ability to lead their institutions through Level-4 transformational change, as described in chapter 1. Like the other strategies presented throughout this book, staff development strategies must be embedded within a well-thought-out and well-executed strategic framework that defines both short- and long-term institutional development paths.

In this chapter, I present a range of strategies, tools, and resources to draw from in order to ensure that staff and faculty are able to expand their knowledge and increase their abilities. The information can be useful to institutional decision makers as they strive to bolster staff development efforts and ensure that those efforts are aligned with—in fact, are an outgrowth of—the institution's core strategies.

WHY STAFF DEVELOPMENT IS IMPORTANT

In summarizing his nationwide survey of faculty development at 250 community colleges, Murray (1999) stated that "with very few exceptions, the colleges surveyed rely on the same activities and programs that two- and four-year colleges have been using for the last 30 to 40 years. The only surprise is why" (p. 59). Why, indeed? Comprehensive staff development means providing support and resources that help employees improve their job performance—which, in turn, is the foundation for improving institutional effectiveness. But if Murray's research is correct, there is a serious problem: If staff development activities were designed for staff and faculty of the 1960s, how can community colleges deliver quality, relevant teaching and service that meet the learning needs of students and the training needs of employers today, nearly half a century later? Since the 1960s the scale and pace of change has quickened to become both amazing and overwhelming. Four types of changes in particular speak to the core importance of staff development activities for community colleges and underscore why college staff and faculty must possess contemporary knowledge and be able to competently perform relevant skills: student populations, technology, staff, and change from an emphasis on teaching to an emphasis on learning. Each area has its own requirements:

- *Changes in student populations:* adaptability and skill to deal with student diversity and widely varying levels of student preparedness (from underpreparedness in basic skills to increased demand for additional training from students with prior postsecondary experience, including bachelor or graduate degrees), flexible teaching styles and learning opportunities, and greater commitment to meeting nonclassroom needs of different student populations.
- *Changes in technology:* ongoing, college-wide learning and technology skill upgrades caused by frequent changes in technology platforms and in college systems and procedures.
- *Changes in staff:* equitable access to training opportunities and equipment for an increasing number of part-time faculty and staff and opportunities that inspire new generations of individuals to fill positions left by the large numbers of retiring faculty, staff, presidents, and board members at community colleges around the country.
- *Change from an emphasis on teaching to an emphasis on learning:* an ability to demonstrate to colleagues, students, and the general public that learning has occurred.

UNDERSTANDING YOUR OWN DEVELOPMENT NEEDS AS A COLLEGE LEADER

Murray's research suggests further that "a climate that fosters and encourages" faculty development is perhaps the most important element of development programs (Murray, 1999, p. 48). He indicated that the primary responsibility for establishing the appropriate climate to expand growth and development lies with the chief academic officer, and he suggested that the college president, as chief academic officer, must model behavior and set expectations that explicitly emphasize the importance of ongoing professional and personal development for all staff.

One of the most effective ways for college presidents to model this type of behavior is to assess their own professional and personal development strengths and challenges. A useful tool for assessing one's own development needs is 360-degree performance feedback. This process relies on feedback from key stakeholders to help leaders understand how they relate to others, identify their strongest assets, and recognize areas in which changes in their skills and abilities might enhance their professional and personal development.

Another valuable staff development resource for college presidents is the President's Academy, sponsored by the American Association of Community Colleges. Events associated with the academy, such as summer institutes, provide structured time for renewal and growth through interaction among presidents. Other organizations also sponsor executive leadership and development programs, such as the League for Innovation in Community Colleges, the American Association of Community College Trustees, and the National Institute for Leadership Development, which emphasizes leadership development for women.

PLANNING FOR COMPREHENSIVE STAFF DEVELOPMENT

Comprehensive staff development programs are an important tool for promoting lifelong learning among college employees. One of the challenges to establishing comprehensive staff development programs is the lack of research about how to best meet the development needs of all levels of staff, not just faculty. There is ample information in the literature about faculty development and how it is intended to enhance teaching. Recently, some researchers have examined how faculty development improves learning and how it can be proved that these activities enhance learning. Information about faculty development may be helpful for identifying development issues and success, but it seems to reinforce traditional beliefs that only full-time faculty have a role in enhancing teaching. However, as colleges move from thinking about better teaching to thinking about better learning, they must reassess the development needs of all college personnel, including administrative staff, board members, and faculty.

Staff development planning and coordination is probably most easily assigned as a responsibility of a functional unit or of at least one specific staff member. This can be an important first step in declaring college-wide commitment and support for staff development. Key issues to consider in the initial planning stages of a comprehensive staff development strategy include the following:

- How should current and emerging institutional staff development needs be identified? What processes should be used for identifying and coordinating technical or subject-specific training needs?
- Should responsibility for staff development be assigned to functional areas rather than to a central staff development unit?
- How should competing staff development needs, such as faculty and nonteaching staff, and full- and part-time faculty and staff, be balanced?
- How will the college pay for staff development activities (cost of external experts, institutional costs of staff being away from work responsibilities)?
- How will staff development planning be integrated into institutional planning processes?
- How will staff development opportunities be promoted, and how will the support of managers and supervisors be secured so that they stress the value of these activities to their staff?

- Should some training be mandatory for all staff, and if not, how should participation be encouraged among staff who may need certain types of training but who may be reluctant to participate?
- What is the best way to offer and expand technology training?
- How will it be determined which resources—whether internal or external—are chosen to deliver staff development training?

Perhaps the most important step in ensuring comprehensive staff development is making decisions about how to assess the success of these programs and activities. Just as community colleges must do a better job of assessing student learning outcomes, they also must assess the learning that is fostered through staff development and training. This requires establishing goals for the training as part of staff development planning. It also requires that the success of training and development activities be monitored through course evaluations and follow-up surveys and measures. Unless the success and effects of training are monitored, staff development activities may quickly become dated and ineffective.

Institutional Example

Some community colleges have improved linkages with nearby universities for both the benefit of student transfer and faculty and staff development. A long-term professional development collaboration between Cuyahoga Community College and Kent State University (KSU), both in Ohio, has resulted in 70 staff members taking KSU courses, with 25 admitted to doctoral programs. (Anglin, cited in Alfano, 1994)

IDENTIFYING STAFF DEVELOPMENT NEEDS

Community college staff development activities fall into three broad categories: college-wide training pertinent to all staff, specific technical or topical training needed to ensure the ongoing expertise of faculty and other staff responsible for operating or supporting equipment and systems, and training and development activities for college trustees and board members. College leaders may face a lack of interest in or even opposition to their staff development plans. For example, opposition may come from managers and supervisors who are reluctant to allow staff members to participate in activities that they see as unrelated to the skills required to do their job. Often, the distinction is made between "hard" or technical skills and "soft skills," which are areas that do not address a technical or advanced area of knowledge. One training consultant put it this way: "I have to laugh when I hear the term 'soft skills.' There is nothing 'soft' about learning how to communicate, how to give constructive feedback or how to negotiate with unions, employees or customers. These are hard skills—the most difficult skills an employee has to learn" (Ganzel, 2001, p. 56).

College-Wide Training

College-wide training is important for fostering institutional values, establishing the legitimacy and importance of new initiatives, and communicating changes in policies, procedures, and systems. Creating opportunities for all college staff to come together, or for smaller groups of staff from different functional areas to participate together in training, builds bridges between employees and work units. This, in turn, can promote a sense of community, something that staff often lament has suffered as colleges have expanded in enrollment, in number and types of programs and courses offered, in locations of course delivery, and in the growth of distance education technologies. As institutions around the country face an expected, dramatic turnover in staff in the coming years, strengthening the sense of "community" in community colleges is vital. The following are some areas of training that leading community colleges have found to be useful:

Customer service training. Each employee has a role in marketing and selling the college. The college's constituents expect that through the daily interactions of college staff with students and other stakeholders, each staff member will embody the attitude and beliefs of the college. Customer service training can help staff improve the quality of customer service at all levels of the college, from the president's office, to academic departments, to the student affairs office, to the corporate training department, and to the maintenance staff.

Diversity training. Every college should be working to ensure that all students and staff are treated equitably and fairly, with respect for differences and appreciation of how differences contribute to improving our colleges. Diversity training can provide faculty and staff with a vocabulary and set of procedures that allow for the acceptance and celebration of diversity. It also provides colleges with the tools and resources to create policies that allow for fair resolution of conflicts arising from diversity issues and to avoid potential legal liability resulting from such conflicts.

Conflict management and resolution. Each incidence of school or workplace violence underscores the urgent need for conflict management. In addition to crises of violence on our campuses, increased staff and student diversity can mean that more instances of butting heads may occur as people with different communication and problem-solving styles come into contact with each other.

Time management. This is a simple yet vital training area for staff, because of increased demands for college programs and services in an environment of diminishing resources and louder calls for public accountability.

New employee orientation. With any job, first-day impressions are important. How employees are treated their first day or week sends a message of how they will be treated throughout their tenure at a college. New employee orientation helps to ensure that new employees get started with the right information and the right attitude from day one. Colleges cannot afford to risk the loss of productivity resulting from the lack of training and orientation; they will lose good employees to other colleges or employers.

Computer and technology training. The never-ending upgrades to existing technology and development of new technology mandate constant training. In addition to training for new technology, further training may be needed if implementing new computer systems results in changes to processes and procedures. An emphasis on technology training should not mean a trade-off that results in declines in other development activities. One step may be to establish a college-wide standard for expected annual staff development hours. The standard could specify the maximum percentage of annual hours that could be dedicated to technology training.

Specific or Topical Training

Faculty training. Specific training is needed to ensure the ongoing technical expertise of faculty and other staff responsible for operating or supporting equipment and systems. Faculty training has traditionally received the most emphasis. In today's environment, staff development programs should focus on the needs of part-time as well as full-time faculty. According to the U.S. Department of Education, 65% of faculty at two-year colleges nationwide are employed part-time (Burnett, 2000). Therefore, part-time faculty training needs, especially, must not be overlooked.

Institutional Example

At the College of the Canyons [Santa Clarita, CA], the majority of faculty are part-time or adjunct instructors with little or no training in teaching. The college has instituted an Associate Program for Adjunct Instructors consisting of four steps: (1) obtaining a department chair's recommendation after completing a minimum of one semester of college service, (2) completing the Instructional Skills Workshop training series, (3) completing an 8- to 10-hour Advanced Teaching Workshop which examines questioning techniques, writing across the curriculum, and critical thinking, and (4) undergoing a classroom evaluation by colleagues and/or students. Completers are advanced in rank to Adjunct Associate Instructor, with a 10% salary increase and a program stipend. (Gerda, 1991, cited in Alfano, 1994)

Several other areas are important for faculty training:

- Understanding new initiatives that emphasize student learning and what these college-wide initiatives mean for each instructor's teaching and learning strategies
- Conducting student assessments, both for entering students to ensure appropriate course and program placements, and as part of ongoing classroom activities to measure the extent to which learning has occurred
- Using information technology—such as curriculum design tools, online courses, and e-mail discussion groups—as part of the overall teaching-learning process
- Improving the teaching-learning process to meet the needs of diverse student populations that include students with ESL needs, students of various ethnicities and ages, students of varying levels of college preparedness (from students with advanced degrees to underprepared students), and students with mental health issues
- Keeping up to date on new research, knowledge, technology, and skills in industries and at universities important to the community or region in which the community college is located

Institutional Examples

The Activating Learning in the Classroom Project at Middlesex Community College is a year-long instructional and professional development program. Eight professors representing each college division volunteer to reconfigure one of their courses to promote active learning. The program begins at the end of the spring semester with five full days of seminars during which the professors assess their own teaching style, their students' thinking, and the materials used in their class. Weekly seminars are continued in the fall and each professor produces a course guide containing a course description, goals and objectives, a detailed syllabus and a large section of reading and focus questions. (Jones & Duffy, 1991, cited in Alfano, 1994)

A freshman retention project at Borough of Manhattan Community College (BMCC) combined faculty development training with curricular reform and counseling changes to reduce high attrition rates in a predominantly minority student population. The BMCC plan included more bilingual hiring, increased community outreach, special programs and workshops on cross-cultural understanding and inter-group dynamics for faculty and staff, a mentoring program for black students, and a special seminar to assist women and minority faculty to complete their doctoral dissertations. Outcomes included increases in student retention, multi-cultural awareness, minority hires, and faculty completion of doctoral degrees. (Kappner, 1991, cited in Alfano, 1994)

Brevard Community College has promoted a particular program of faculty professional development for several years called the Return to Industry (RTI) program. Faculty from any discipline who are interested in updating their skills and knowledge of new technology can propose 4- to 6-week summer projects at industry sites of their choice. Participating faculty receive a modest stipend and can receive credit towards the graduate coursework hours required in the union contract. (Layne, 1991, cited in Alfano, 1994)

Non-faculty training. Non-faculty staff members also have specific training needs. Training areas to consider for non-faculty staff include the following:

- Understanding how new imperatives for student learning affect college-wide support services, including staff-student interactions, and the various ways in which support services are delivered
- Using technology, particularly information technology, to make operations more effective and efficient
- Improving the college workplace culture through diversity training that addresses the needs of diverse staff and student populations

Emerging development needs for staff with supervisory and hiring responsibilities reflect changes in student and staff populations, in the types of programs and services provided, and in how they are provided. Specialized training in this area becomes especially important in light of recent court cases indicating that institutions may be held liable for illegal behavior of their staff and, in some cases, students. Training areas to consider for these employees include the following:

- Determining the types of learning activities that will most effectively enhance each employee's performance
- Monitoring and evaluating progress in meeting job performance expectations
- Identifying root causes of problem performance and developing appropriate responses that will help employees and protect the college from future litigation
- Coaching employees
- Understanding diversity
- Carrying out fair and effective employee performance appraisals
- Making hiring decisions that reflect the attributes important to the college environment

College Trustees and Board Members

Community college presidents must help their boards understand the importance of their own professional and personal development. Some trustees may have only limited awareness and knowledge of community college career and education issues, board functions under policy governance, or government fiscal and budget requirements and practices. Trustees can benefit from regularly scheduled learning activities that focus on broad college initiatives, new topics, or trends in postsecondary education. A college president, working with the board chair, can inform and sometimes form the perspectives and viewpoints of college trustees. Emphasizing development opportunities for college boards sends an important message to other members of the college community about the value of learning for all stakeholders. Here are some suggestions for identifying and delivering trustee development activities:

- Survey trustees about areas in which they would like training, asking them to rank their interest on a list of possible topics.
- Develop an annual board orientation seminar.
- Work with the board chair to include board development as part of annual board goals.
- Invite board members to participate in staff development activities offered for college employees, such as college-wide gatherings or dialogues that may occur once or twice a year; regularly scheduled training courses in topics such as effectiveness, diversity, and values; and special staff development workshops or presentations.

STAFF DEVELOPMENT FORMATS

Traditionally, staff development includes workshops and training sessions that may range from a few hours to several days. Training and workshops might be provided on site by internal or external staff, or staff might travel to attend training sessions somewhere else. These activities are still the predominant method for providing staff development. Traditional workshops and training sessions may be most appropriate when using staff development as a method to communicate about new initiatives or issues, or to establish a common set of expectations about how colleges operate or perform their daily work.

Another traditional staff development activity for faculty is the use of sabbaticals, which some institutions make available to all staff. Conferences are much shorter and less costly to the institution than sabbaticals. Like sabbaticals, however, conference attendance typically benefits only a small number of college staff. For both, college leaders must think about establishing criteria that help define when participation is appropriate. Other issues related

to sabbaticals and conferences include determining how a sabbatical or conference participation will benefit the broader college community (e.g., through reporting on activities or
offering workshops based on knowledge or expertise gained during the sabbatical); the
appropriate length of sabbaticals or frequency of conference attendance; and how sabbatical
costs, such as paid leave and replacement staff, will be covered (through a central fund,
individual functional units, foundation grants, and so forth).

Other activities, such as cross-functional training, partnering with other colleges, or
partnering with business and industry, can be structured as staff development opportunities,
too. Each activity has issues and questions that college leaders should consider. For instance,
cross-functional training expands the knowledge base of staff who become familiar with
new activities or other operational units. It contributes to efficient operations by increasing
organizational flexibility for responding to staffing changes or fluctuations in demands for
college services. College leaders should consider the possible impact on collective bargaining
agreements. They also should consider who will evaluate staff performance and who will
determine staffing assignments for cross-functional training.

Partnering with other colleges can be a useful tool for expanding staff development
resources. For example, if a nearby college brings in a national speaker, a partnering agree-
ment to help share the presentation cost may be beneficial to both institutions. Another type
of partnering involves the exchange of staff. This can provide excellent staff development by
allowing employees to experience how another college operates. Besides gaining new knowledge, exchanges often promote positive feelings about what is occurring within the partici-
pant's own college.

Business and industry partnerships can provide hands-on staff development. Through
these partnerships, faculty could spend an agreed-upon amount of time actually doing the
type of work for which they are training their students. Staff working in administrative support functions could work in a similar function for a private business. This type of partnering
helps a college reach out to its stakeholders and provides good exposure for its employees.

ATTRACTING, DEVELOPING, AND RETAINING FACULTY AND STAFF

Nothing is more important to college leaders than the ability to attract and employ good
people, develop them well, and retain them. Consider that a single faculty member will cost
an average of $50,000 per year. Over a 25-year period that faculty member will cost
$1,250,000. Yet he or she will produce an average of $70,000 of revenue per year, yielding
$1,875,000 over 25 years. In spite of technological advances, people are still a college's
most important resource.

The first step to attracting good staff and faculty is to establish this as a high priority.
College leaders should begin by answering these five fundamental questions:

- Do we select our employees with the same degree of diligence that we select our
  equipment?
- Do we have a reputation for being employee-focused?
- Do we have an effective supply chain of new employees (that is, do we have good relationships with high schools, colleges, one-stop career centers, employers, and other
  organizations that may provide sources from which to recruit our staff and faculty)?

- Do we provide better incentives than our competition?
- Do our faculty and staff reflect the diversity of our student population?

If the answer to all five questions is yes, then the college in question is truly unique. In most cases, the answer to one or more of the questions is no; therefore, administrators, supervisors, and human resource professionals have a fine opportunity for growth in the recruiting area.

Many colleges are enjoying successful recruiting because they have made the choice to focus on solutions rather than on the problem. These colleges establish great reputations for supporting their employees; establish a worker supply chain; and provide competitive incentives, such as good benefits, a merit-based compensation system, and ample opportunities for training and learning.

Developing a worker supply chain is a relatively new phenomenon for colleges. The most successful efforts have been those in which the college partners with local workforce preparation programs, high schools, community colleges, technical colleges, and universities. Providing scholarships, internships, and cooperative education opportunities, and assisting with program advisory committees are effective methods of establishing a ready supply of emerging workers.

Because of the diversity of the student body today, community colleges must ensure that their worker supply chains include organizations that can provide a pool of candidates for faculty and staff positions that will reflect the diversity of the student population.

> According to recent studies (Carter, 1994), approximately 90% of the total faculty at the nation's two- and four-year, public and private colleges are white. The highest percentage of faculty of color is employed at public four-year institutions (12.6%), a figure influenced by the inclusion of historically black colleges. The lowest percentage is employed at private two-year colleges (2.6%). In studies conducted between 1988 and 1992, 3–5.1% of the faculty at two-year colleges were African American, 1–1.4% were American Indian, 2–2.2% were Asian American, 1.7% were Mexican American, 0.2–0.3% were Puerto Rican American. In comparison with all two-year college faculty, faculty of color are somewhat less likely to have a master's degree, more likely to have tenure, and very close to the national median for salary.
>
> Opp and Smith's (1994) study of the recruitment and retention of minority faculty highlighted a number of institutional factors that served as predictors of whether a college had a high percentage of under-represented minorities on the faculty. Predictors influencing both recruitment and retention included having an African American, Mexican American or American Indian vice president of academic affairs; the amount of contact that vice presidents of academic affairs had with minority students and faculty; and having minorities serving on college boards of trustees. (Colby & Foote, 1995)

Owens, Reis, and Hall (1994, cited in Colby & Foote, 1995) and Nicholas and Oliver (1995, cited in Colby & Foote, 1995) suggested a variety of ways in which community colleges can be more effective in their efforts to recruit and retain minority:

Recruitment

- Ensure a commitment to institutional diversity from the highest levels of college administration.
- Keep an open mind in evaluating the credentials of minority candidates, and recognize the value of nonacademic experiences.
- Include minority professionals from the service area on search committees.
- Utilize minority media in recruitment campaigns, especially when language is an important factor.
- Make use of partnerships with business and industry to seek out potential candidates.
- Initiate programs that aggressively seek well-qualified minority candidates and women through wide varieties of networks and personal contacts.
- Include minority members on interview committees.
- Keep candidate pools open until minority and female candidates with appropriate credentials are found.
- Maintain ongoing dialogues and faculty exchanges with historically Black colleges.
- Implement long-range programs that encourage minority and women students from elementary school through graduate programs.
- Diversify administration, staff, and student bodies as well as faculties.

Retention

- Begin with a thorough orientation, and provide assistance with college and campus resources, housing, shopping, and community services.
- Schedule activities that require all faculty to interact, such as diversity training and staff development programs to promote collegiality.
- Incorporate minority faculty into the decision-making process of the college, mainstream the teaching assignments, and include them in all facets of campus life and activities.

Institutional Example

The Maricopa Community Colleges used many of these recruitment strategies in their efforts to create applicant pools in which minorities and women are well represented. They visited colleges with large minority populations, produced direct mailings sent to individual minority graduate students, and sent faculty representatives to state and district minority organizations. These efforts resulted in an increase in full-time minority faculty, from 127 professors in 1987 (16.2% of the total) to 176 professors in 1992 (19.2%). They have also increased the number of minority managers (deans, directors, and coordinators) from 66 in 1987 (19.6%) to 91 in 1992 (23.2%). (adapted from Colby & Foote, 1995)

Colleges must provide strong incentives to attract and retain the highest quality candidates, regardless of ethnic background, religious background, or gender. Providing finder's fees for new hire referrals is a good incentive for existing employees, but direct recruitment incentives generally bring the best return. The following incentives are common among leading businesses and community colleges:

- Personal services, such as day care, fitness centers, dry cleaning, and transportation
- Growth opportunities, such as travel, professional development, college tuition
- Good environment
- Skill certification training
- Immediate team membership and instant recognition
- Competitive pay and benefits
- Flexible work schedules

Supporting employees also includes investing in their future. Today's workers want to know if they will have career growth opportunities. It is up to college leaders to provide those professional development activities through relevant training, conferences, and seminars. "But if we keep training them, competitors might steal them away from us" is a common refrain. Is it better to train people and risk losing them, or not train them and keep them?

All of the foregoing suggestions are people-centered. Employees are more than great assets, they are stakeholders in the organization. Not only do they need to know the expectations of their leaders, their leaders need to know their employees' expectations and dreams as well. Some visionary organizations are establishing "expectation agreements" or "goal matching understandings" with all new and existing employees. Colleges could use this same technique. The idea is to discover connections between employee goals and company goals. When employees realize that they can reach their personal goals by helping the company reach its goals, productivity increases. The residual benefits include a better understanding of employee needs and company expectations, better communication, and mutual trust. Employees feel valued and feel that they are part of the team. Conversely, if employees' perceptions of the company and its values are different from their expectations, tension will arise that will often lead to poor performance or separation.

CONCLUSION

Perhaps the most important thing to remember about staff development is that we must challenge ourselves, our faculty, and our staff to meet or exceed the same standard of lifelong learning that we expect for our students. All college stakeholders, from trustees to part-time clerks and custodians, are being dramatically affected by the rapid changes in student populations, changes in technology, and changes in staffing through retirements and increases in the number of part-time faculty and staff. Making comprehensive staff development an institutional priority is essential if community colleges are to maintain reputations of excellence.

References

Alfano, K. (1994, March). *Recent strategies for faculty development.* Los Angeles: ERIC Clearinghouse for Community Colleges. (ED371807)

Burnett, S. (2000, June 26). Part-time teachers, full-time problems. *Community College Week, 12.*

Colby, A., & Foote, E. (1995, July). *Creating and maintaining a diverse faculty.* Los Angeles: ERIC Clearinghouse for Community Colleges. (ED386261)

Ganzel, R. (2001). Hard training for soft skills. *Training, 38.*

Manske, F. A. (1999). *Secrets of effective leadership: A practical guide to success.* Columbia, TN: Leadership Education and Development.

Murray, J. P. (1999). Faculty development in a national sample of community colleges. *Community College Review, 27*(3).

Chapter 9

RESOURCE CAPACITY DEVELOPMENT

Gunder Myran

Presidents, provosts, chief financial officers, and other campus leaders must form a strategic alliance to map and guide the course of change. . . . The revolution must start at the top.

—Rodney Napier, C. Clinton Sidle, Patrick Sanaghan, and William S. Reed (1998)

The purpose of this chapter is to articulate the role of the community college president and executive team in building and managing the capacities or resources of the college to achieve its mission, vision, and core strategies. Using the definition of strategic leadership in chapter 1, building and managing the community college's capacity is clearly one of the primary execution strategies. One of the most important ways the president and executive team can align the institution's core strategies to their execution is through building and managing human resources, financial resources, physical resources, information resources, and goodwill or reputation of the college. The community college executive leader's role is to build and manage the organization's capacity so as to have maximum impact on achieving its mission and strategies.

BUILDING FINANCIAL CAPACITY

A vital area of capacity building is the building and management of the college's financial resources. Having adequate funds to achieve the college's mission and strategies does not alone ensure success, but it represents an essential building block. Primary strategic elements of financial leadership include the following:

- Building relationships with legislators and government bodies that influence and allocate the local, state, and federal funds available to the college
- Building relationships with foundation officials and private-sector donors whose philanthropic priorities relate to the mission of the community college
- Developing mission-centered programs and services that relate to the funding priorities of legislative bodies, foundations, and private-sector donors

- Building relationships with community leaders who will serve as advocates for the community college's interests when funding allocation decisions are being made by public and private bodies
- For community colleges that depend on local property tax or other local tax revenues, leading a continuous campaign to build the awareness and support of local taxpayers and voters for the college's mission and achievements
- Providing overall leadership of millage renewal and increase campaigns, keeping in mind that such campaigns are a referendum on the reputation and success of the college in the community over time. A clever campaign is unlikely to overcome a bad reputation or neglect of community educational needs, but a good reputation and a strong record of effective community service are the essential building blocks for a successful campaign.
- Developing a long-term financial strategy
- Designing and leading the annual action planning and budget cycle
- Leading an annual program review process
- Developing the private fundraising capacity of the college

Developing a Long-Term Financial Strategy

The driving force of a long-range financial strategy is student success, community success, faculty and staff success, operational excellence, and organizational learning and growth strategies that are encompassed in the college's strategic framework. The purpose of the financial strategy is to align the way that financial resources of the college are developed and managed to the achievement of the college's mission and its program and service strategies.

A component of this planning process is a periodically updated, 10-year "financial map" that outlines revenue and expenditure trends based on a set of articulated assumptions about financial aspects such as state aid, local property taxes, student enrollments, future faculty and staff profiles and costs, and program and service trends. The 10-year financial map identifies long-range areas of concern based on the stated assumptions. For example, if the 10-year revenue and expenditure assumptions indicate a deficit situation in Year 5 and beyond, the college leadership has an opportunity to consider revenue and expenditure strategies that will remedy this situation before that time arrives.

It may be well to develop five or more financial maps based on different assumptions. In this way, the college executive leadership can decide which assumptions have sufficient merit to justify action. The main advantage of a long-term look at financial trends, even though there are many unknown factors, is that leaders have the leverage of time to make revenue and expenditure adjustments that anticipate future conditions. The 10-year financial map permits leaders to assume certain major instructional program, service, or technology outcomes based on the strategic framework, and then leverage year-by-year financial decisions over a period of time to provide the human, financial, and physical capacity to achieve the desired outcomes.

Another component of the long-term financial strategy is the 5-year financial plan. The 5-year financial plan is far more detailed than the 10-year financial map, but is an outgrowth of the assumptions and revenue and expenditure projections of the map. The 5-year financial plan can be seen as a 5-year budget in the sense that it is detailed enough, especially for the first two or three years, to serve as the foundation for annual budget development.

The purpose of the 5-year financial plan is to address in detail the financial resources required to produce the outcomes outlined in the strategic framework and to ensure that each annual budget is designed to secure the revenues and make expenditure decisions that move the college in the direction of achieving those outcomes. The 5-year financial plan, or 5-year budget, gives the college leaders the leverage of time to orchestrate revenue and expenditure decisions to achieve certain ends that would not be possible with a one-year perspective. As an example, suppose the college recognizes that within three years a new information system will need to be installed at a cost of $8 million. A 5-year financial plan permits the leadership to anticipate this need, perhaps in this case building a reserve for this purpose over a three-year period.

Annual Action Planning and Budget Cycle

The annual action plan is the tactical expression of how the outcomes outlined in the strategic framework of the college will be accomplished during a 12-month period. If there is no annual action plan, the annual budget becomes the plan by default. The annual action plan states in specific, measurable terms what will be accomplished during the coming year to move toward producing the outcomes of the strategic framework.

The annual action plan also serves as a guide to administrators and faculty members as they work with their supervisors to detail their individual annual performance plans. The financial resources of the college then provide the capacity to realize these institutional and individual plans. In that sense, the annual budget is the tool that permits the college, its various units, and individual faculty and staff members to activate their plans and dreams. Many colleges, for example, include in their annual budget funds to be allocated specifically to enable administrators and faculty members to carry out their individual performance plans.

A number of community colleges use some form of zero-based budgeting or 90%-based budgeting to signal that certain funds allocated in the previous year will be reexamined prior to allocation for the current year. Suppose that a 90%-based budgeting process is used, where units receive 90% of last year's allocation and the remaining 10% goes into a reservoir for reallocation to the highest priority needs dictated by the strategic framework and the annual action plan. In such a budget allocation process, there are winners and losers. However, the extremely important strategic message is that, in a period of rapid environmental change, the college cannot operate on a business as usual basis. Each year, priorities must change, and some older programs and services must give way to emerging demands and new programming and services.

Annual Program Review Process

It is very painful to eliminate or reduce programs, services, or other functions of the college, because this may have a negative impact on the jobs and careers of faculty and staff members. However, the integrity of the college's mission and financial strategies demands an annual program review process through which selected instructional programs, administrative functions, and student services are evaluated for their currency, effectiveness, and alignment with the college's mission.

An annual program review process is also the appropriate format to make decisions regarding elimination, reduction, continuation, or expansion of specific programs, services, and functions. In cases where programs are reduced or eliminated, the financial resources released can then be reallocated to higher priority needs as part of a responsible financial management program. To reduce the negative impact of displacement of faculty and staff, many community colleges offer reassignment and retraining opportunities. Although this is important, it is equally important that faculty and staff members not be reassigned to positions for which they are marginally prepared, lest future generations of students suffer from the resulting mediocre teaching or service.

A good example of program review is provided by the experience of the California community colleges during the cost-cutting period of the 1990s (Burstein, 1996). Cost-cutting steps included reduction of personnel, increases in average class size, reduction in the number of sections of courses offered, and reallocation of funds from one program to another.

Private Fundraising Capacity

Community college foundations are largely a phenomenon of recent decades. This private fundraising arm of the college, usually operated as a nonprofit corporation, is a partner with the college leadership in raising funds for student scholarships, instructional equipment, capital projects, and other initiatives that meet the special philanthropic interests of the donors. Building the college's private fundraising capacity involves several strategic elements.

Use the foundation as a mechanism for "friend raising." Many community college leaders feel that the friend-raising function of a community college foundation is equal in importance to fundraising. Through the fundraising efforts of the foundation, the college can create relationships with community leaders and donors that might not be possible through any other mechanism. This friend-raising process, of course, often leads to fundraising in progressively larger amounts. The tendency of donors to increase their giving as they get to know the college and its financial needs better is an insight to be nurtured by the executive team. The deeper connection of donors to the college can also pay other dividends as these college supporters interact with their peers in the community and influence their thinking about the college.

Use the proceeds of fundraising by the foundation to create an "edge of excellence." It is important that funds raised privately not be used for remedying operating budget shortfalls. Other financial mechanisms, such as program and staff reduction and budget reallocation, should be used for this purpose. This is important for two reasons. First, donors want to contribute to a successful organization. Donors are reluctant to bail out a college that seems to be struggling, and crying poverty is unlikely to speak to their philanthropic objectives. Second, private funds should be used to create an edge of excellence for the college. These funds should be invested in high-impact, highly visible projects, such as student scholarships, special services for low-income students, capital projects, and faculty excellence awards that are beyond the capacity of the operating budget. One payoff of this approach comes when student recipients of foundation scholarships share their stories at a scholarship luncheon to which donors are invited. Many community college leaders have observed tears all around the room as these stories of courage in the face of hardship are shared, only to realize that they themselves have moist eyes and a lump in their throats as well.

Use the foundation to increase direct involvement of community leaders. Many community leaders will not agree to serve on the college's board of trustees, especially if they must run an election campaign, but will agree to be appointed to the foundation's board of directors. Most board members develop an affection for the college as they learn more about its mission and especially its open-door commitment. As this process unfolds, they are more likely to become major donors and to serve as advocates for the college in the community. As the board members end their terms of office, the college builds an ever-increasing number of ex-board members who support the college in their community interactions.

Participate in major fundraising efforts. The president and, to some extent, the members of the executive team, play an important role in fundraising. As was noted, the president plays an important role in building relationships with potential major donors. It is, however, a truism that major donors give to major donors. Although the president can play an important relationship-building role, an established major donor can better ask another potential donor to contribute. One reason for this is that the president may be seen by some as having self-interest in securing additional funds for the college, untrue as this may be. More important, this is the community's college, and it is appropriate that those from the community should invite others to contribute to the college in the same way that they have.

DEVELOPMENT OF THE PHYSICAL CAPACITY OF THE COLLEGE

The facilities that house college operations are vital resources for achieving the college's mission and strategies, as are the sites on which these operations are located. The facilities and sites are assets of the college, not only because they house its programs, services, and other functions, but also because they express the character and image of the college—traditional or contemporary, open or closed, formal or informal. Some have referred to the facilities as the "frozen art" of the college because they stand as beacons for all to see and to form opinions about.

The opinions the college's stakeholders form about the quality and appearance of the facilities translate into opinions about the college itself. A community college near a university would be making, for example, a very clear statement if its facilities were inferior to those of the university. The public would be quite likely to equate the quality of the facilities with the quality of the programs and services that they house. The ongoing development of the college's facilities is also important because of the constant need to modify and renovate spaces in response to changing educational and technological requirements. Leadership of facility and site development involves several strategic elements.

Periodic assessment of changing community educational needs and changes in the programs and services of the college, and the implications for space and facility improvement projects. The driving force for any facility improvement projects should be changing educational needs of the students and community.

Regular updates of a facility master plan and the site development master plan. Using the services of a professional architectural firm, the executive team should provide leadership in identifying future facility and site development needs and specifying specific new construction, renovation, and major repair projects that are required in the years ahead. The facility master plan should include a space organization plan that outlines the future functions of each building and the interrelations of these functions in terms of adjacency. When new facilities are built, a wonderful opportunity is created to rethink the functions of existing buildings in light of changing needs, especially in the case of buildings in which there will be vacated spaces as a result of the move of certain functions to a new building.

Building support for new facilities and the remodeling, renovation, and repair projects contained in the master plans. Support must be gained from members of the board of trustees, faculty and staff, community leaders, legislators, and government officials if these projects are to become a reality.

Developing a capital budget and securing financial resources to execute the facility and site master plans. The master facility and site master plans are the levers for seeking funds for future projects. These projects must be compelling from a political as well as an educational perspective. For example, to secure state funding, it is probably better to propose a facility devoted to career education than one intended for student fitness and recreation. The funding approach could include the issuing of revenue-anticipation bonds based on planned operating budget reserves, a campaign to seek voter approval to issue construction bonds, seeking of state and federal funds, a private fundraising campaign, or any combination of these approaches.

Selection of design teams. The selection of architects and engineers to design facility and site development projects is a very important step. This design team will be a partner with the college leadership in creating a facility that will project the desired image of the college, house programs and services in an effective and future-oriented way, and provide for flexibility as these programs and services change.

Determination of construction methods. For simpler projects, the general contractor method is usually preferred. In this case, the design team directs the project, although both the architect and the general contractor report to the college. For more complex projects, colleges often add a construction management firm to represent the college's interests and to monitor the progress of the project.

BUILDING THE INFORMATION CAPACITY OF THE COLLEGE

Information is a vital resource of the community college. The processes by which information is generated, shared, and used form a web of interactions that determines the pace of the daily life of the college. Consider what happens, for example, when the semester class schedule is late in getting back from the printer. An array of college systems grinds to a halt because vital information is lacking on which these systems depend. As community colleges increase the use of e-mail, the Internet, and Web sites, the flow of information grows ever faster, more complex, and more voluminous. Information in various forms and from a great variety of sources around the world now bombards the college daily. The expansion and increasing complexity of information flow creates both opportunities and challenges for the strategic leadership of the community college. The executive team can contribute to the development of the college's information resources in several ways.

Emphasize dialogue among stakeholder groups. Dialogue is the primary way that the college conducts its business and builds its culture. Although face-to-face dialogue is important for both information sharing and relationship building, dialogue can be significantly enhanced through the use of e-mail, teleconferencing, and other forms of electronic communication. It is through dialogue with internal and community groups that the community college leader gains the information and insights needed to make high-quality strategic decisions. Dialogue is also the way the leader develops an in-depth understanding of the college's mission, vision, and strategies among faculty and staff groups, such that they will have this foundation as they make decisions and take daily actions.

Provide financial support for the college's information systems. One of the most rapidly growing areas of expenditure for community college management is staffing and improvement of the information system. The installation of new management information systems, the vastly expanding use of the college's Web site, expansion of campus networking, the installation of various types of software, and the provision of computers to individual faculty and staff members, all have moved the college to a new level of information processing and communication that would have been impossible to achieve without this technology. Because of its critical importance, the development and management of information systems must be given a high priority in the college's strategic and annual financial strategies.

Use forms of "invisible leadership." The leader cannot always be present with various groups to communicate the college's character, mission, vision, and strategies. The creative use of banners, posters, brochures, advertisements, and other means of invisible leadership can convey these central messages 24 hours a day, 7 days a week. Many community colleges, for example, have posted these fundamental statements in each classroom. When a major strategic initiative is undertaken, hallway posters can be used to announce the initiative. Community colleges increasingly use billboards to achieve this same purpose in the community, as well as making traditional use of various media.

Manage by walking around. Although "management by walking around" has been somewhat discredited because of the disingenuous way it was used by some leaders, informal contact with students, faculty, and staff in the hallways, lunch rooms, lobbies, and classrooms of the campus is still a good tool for information sharing and relationship building. The leader cannot get a true feel for what is really happening around campus without being there. Many community college leaders are grateful for insights they gained while walking around that averted a crisis or improved the quality of a decision.

BUILDING GOODWILL AND REPUTATION

One of the assets of a business enterprise is goodwill: the reputation of the business among its customers and other constituencies. Goodwill is an important factor when the selling price of a business is being determined, because this adds to or detracts from the value of the business in the eyes of the buyer. Similarly, the goodwill or reputation of a community college is an extremely valuable asset or resource that affects the institution in many ways: the decision of a potential student to enroll, the decision of a business to use the college for the customized training of its employees, the interest of donors in contributing funds to the college, and the interest of community organizations in partnering with the college in shared ventures. Strengthening the reputation of the college and protecting this valuable resource are an essential strategic role of the president and the executive team. Leadership in this area is achieved in several ways.

Build relationships with community leaders, groups, and organizations. Relationship building is at the center of all efforts to enhance and protect the reputation of the college. Through personal relationships, college executives can keep key constituencies informed about changing college circumstances and can take the pulse of the community with regard to changing perceptions of the institution.

Lead a marketing and public relations program. Marketing here is defined as continuously assessing the gap between the changing educational needs of the community and the actual programs and services of the college, and then working to close that gap through program and service development. An effective marketing program is one where there is a perfect match between community educational needs and the programs and services provided by the college. The first step in an effective marketing and public relations program is doing a good job, and the second is telling the community about it. Although billboards, advertisements, and mailings play an important role in telling the college's story, grassroots personal contacts with individuals, groups, and community organizations are likely to have a greater impact on promoting the reputation of the college.

Build a culture of customer service. It is said that when a student or other constituent has a good experience (or a bad experience) at a community college, at least 60 other people hear about it. Obviously, the objective must be to serve students and other customers so well that they tell their friends and associates good news about the college, not bad news. Satisfied students are the best advocates for the college. The accumulation of good news from many satisfied students is far more powerful that any promotional effort. Many community colleges now have faculty and staff professional development programs that provide instruction on customer service. Also, some community colleges have transformed systems such as admissions, registration, and food service to make them more customer-friendly. System changes may include empowering front-line workers, such as counselors and registration clerks, to make judgments about student services that in the past were reserved for higher-level administrators. At one college, for example, student services specialists can make the decision about a student tuition refund up to a certain level, right at the point of service.

Ensure that a crisis management process is in place. When a crisis occurs at the college, the executive leadership must be prepared to deal with the situation expeditiously and forthrightly. Cases of violence, sexual abuse, and other criminal acts, as well as financial irregularities and other internal problems, can severely damage the reputation of the college unless handled properly. A crisis management process must include an emergency plan, a media relations plan, and an internal communications plan. Some colleges have a prearranged location for a crisis center, and all administrators know the steps they are to take to participate in resolving the crisis. (For further discussion of crisis management, see chapter 10.)

BUILDING THE COLLEGE'S HUMAN RESOURCES CAPACITY

No discussion about capacity building in the community college is complete without a review of the central resource, the faculty and staff. The faculty and staff of a community college are an amazingly diverse configuration of professionals that includes artists, technicians, writers, engineers, historians, social workers, radiologists, chemists, office professionals, computer network and programming specialists, biologists, anthropologists, social scientists, mathematicians, nurses, managers, and custodial workers. The common ground for this diverse gathering of professionals is their dedication to student success and to teaching and learning. As such, they represent the most important resources of the college.

Some community college faculty and staff members object to being referred to as "resources," feeling that it is demeaning for human beings to be equated to financial or physical resources. This is a point well taken: faculty, support staff, and administrators are the heartbeat of the college—they *are* the college. However, the terms *human resources* and *human resources management* are so widely used among community college practitioners that they define the processes by which the faculty and staff of the college achieve and maintain a match between their knowledge and skills, and those required in the classrooms, labs, and office of the institution.

Without question, decisions about the hiring and development of professional faculty and staff are among the most important, and expensive, ones college leaders make. This is true for several reasons. First, assuming low turnover, which is the case at most community colleges, it can be assumed that, over the length of a career, a single professional represents a very significant investment. Second, making a bad hiring decision, particularly with regard to faculty, will mean mediocre instruction and service to students. Third, making a bad hiring decision can lead to costly and very time-consuming progressive discipline and dismissal proceedings laced with legal battles. The primary ways in which the president and the executive team provide leadership for human resources development are as follows.

Establish a human resources development system. Human resources development starts with the first recruiting contact with a potential faculty or staff member and ends at retirement or termination. Human resources development includes making potential candidates for vacant positions aware of the college, recruiting, hiring, making contractual arrangements, conducting orientation, arranging compensation levels, assigning duties, conducting professional development, performing evaluations, administering progressive discipline including dismissal, promotions and recognition, and doing retirement planning. Some retirees continue to provide part-time teaching or other services, and many remain members of the college community through attendance at special events or by joining a college retirees' organization.

It is the responsibility of the college executives to be certain that all parts of this system are functioning effectively and that proper financial investments are made in faculty and staff development. It is amazing, given the rapid changes in the workplace, in technology, and in teaching methodologies, that some community colleges pay substantial salaries to hire quality faculty and staff but then do not make the necessary investment to continue to develop them throughout their tenure. Certainly, funding the development of the faculty and staff is one of the most important investments a community college can make.

Create a process of participative management. In today's complex and rapidly changing world, no one person could possibly process all the impulses bombarding the college from the environment, sort out which ones require response, and then take the necessary action. Many faculty and staff members must share the work, steering when their expertise and experience are the most appropriate. The president and executive team must empower faculty and staff groups to participate in institutional decision making, although the appropriate administrator in most cases will be the ultimate decision maker. There are four levels of this participation: notification, consultation, collaboration, and consensus.

First, when the decision maker has all the information and input he or she needs, participation for the faculty and staff takes the form of simply being informed about decisions that have been made. At the second level, the decision maker generally has the information he or she needs to make the decision but wishes to consult with a committee or hold a dialogue session to obtain additional input. After this consultation, the decision maker proceeds to make the decision and share the results with those affected. At the third level, the decision maker charges a faculty or staff committee with making a decision regarding a matter with specified conditions. The committee deliberates and makes a recommendation to the decision maker. The decision maker accepts the recommendation if it meets the specified conditions or returns the recommendation to the committee indicating why it does not meet the conditions. If, ultimately, the committee does not provide a recommendation the decision maker feels meets the specifications, he or she makes the decision but indicates why certain aspects of the recommendation were not accepted. At the fourth level, the decision maker turns a matter over to a committee, indicating that he or she will accept and enact the recommendation of the committee. In a participative form of governance, the ultimate decision makers have a responsibility to move as many decisions as possible toward the "shared" and "committee" decision options just described.

Have the chief human resources development officer report to the president. Given the importance of human resources development to the overall development of the college, the chief human resources officer should report to the president and be a member of the president's executive committee.

Oversee the development and implementation of an annual planning and performance review program for individual faculty and staff. To effectively direct the human resources of the college toward the achievement of the institutional mission and strategies, it is vital that each faculty member and administrator prepare and activate an individual performance plan each year. Without such a program, the most important resource of the college will be without focus and direction, and much of this resource will be wasted or misdirected. Executives should take the lead in developing annual institutional, divisional, and departmental plans based on the outcomes outlined in the strategic framework, and then in turn lead the faculty and staff in developing individual performance plans on this basis. The success of these efforts relies on the involvement of supervisors at all levels and on providing the financial support to empower individuals to carry out their plans.

CONCLUSION

A key strategic leadership role of the community college president and executive team is to continuously increase the capacity of the organization to achieve its best future. The development and management of reputation, human resources, financial resources, physical resources, and information resources in ways that are aligned with the college's mission and strategies requires the in-depth involvement of the president and the executive team.

References

Burstein, M. (1996, August). *The thin green line: Community colleges' struggle to do more with less*. Los Angeles: ERIC Clearinghouse for Community Colleges. (ED400024)

Napier, R., Clinton Sidle, C., Sanaghan, P., & Reed, W. S. (1998). *Metamorphosis: Creating the capacity for change. NACUBO Business Officer, 31*(7).

Part III

SPECIAL STRATEGIC DIMENSIONS

Chapter 10

CRISIS AND CONFLICT MANAGEMENT

Beverly Simone and George A. Baker III

Community Colleges differ from other forms of higher education in ways that have vast implications for leadership.

—Richard C. Richardson, Jr. and Mimi Wolverton

The purpose of this chapter is to present the argument that conflict is inevitable but can be managed and to present theories and concepts to be employed by the president and the leadership team necessary to resolve conflict where it negatively affects morale, essential functioning, and organizational health. It is the responsibility of the president to manage conflict in the most effective manner possible. Conflict poorly managed can become a full-blown crisis, with dire consequences for the institution and for its members. Some threats to the college cannot be predicted or controlled, only managed once they occur. When the president and the senior leadership team work every day to manage conflict effectively, then when unpredictable crises occur, the college will be in a better position to weather the storm and to move into a more stable future.

All sorts of potential crises can affect community colleges and other institutions. How college presidents and leadership teams handle crises is a direct outgrowth of the strategic framework they create, as well as the range of foundational and execution strategies they adopt. This chapter is concerned with how conflict and crisis management and prevention fit within the strategic framework of the institution.

CRISES AT COMMUNITY COLLEGES

There are numerous possible crises that can occur at community colleges:

- A scandal involving college leaders, faculty, or staff
- A natural or manmade catastrophe, such as a fire, flood, tornado, or act of terrorism that destroys college facilities
- A decision by the board of trustees to end the tenure of a president
- A legal challenge to college policies in areas such as admissions, mandatory student fees, affirmative action or diversity, academic (i.e., faculty) freedom of speech, and sunshine laws affecting the accessibility of public records

- A vote of no-confidence by the faculty senate
- Major cuts in state appropriations
- A faculty organization call for a strike
- Failure of databases and information systems, including online and phone registration systems
- Theft
- Violent crime

Crisis within a college might result when management decisions are not well received or are perceived as having been made without widespread input or involvement from staff. For example, the decision by upper college management, including the president and leadership team, to reorganize the college could escalate to crisis if appropriate forethought does not anticipate questions and concerns. Anticipating questions allows other staff to assist in preparing materials to share throughout the college after the initial announcement of such a major change. In fact, planning for post-announcement communication and activities should be an integral part of any discussions about major college changes.

Preceding an event such as a faculty strike or a board decision to end a president's tenure, there may be an unusual, unforeseeable, or unstable situation: a turning point in the life of the president, internal or external political forces readying a challenge to leadership, or faculty hearing word of successful bargaining agreements at other institutions. The same can be said of budget cuts that occur in the middle of the budget year or a take-back of 5% directed by the governor and the state legislature. In all likelihood, the political events leading up to the mandated take-back will have been developing for a considerable period of time.

In this chapter we present theories and concepts designed to help college leaders deal with conflict and crises in general and then describe some strategies that presidents and their executive teams can use to deal with them. Crises that are foreseeable, based on an honest assessment of institutional history, decisions made by past and current leaders, and other factors, will provide a foundation for the general discussion and review of proven organizational concepts. Other crises, such as a vote of no-confidence, a board's decision to end the tenure of a president, legal challenges, faculty strikes, and state budget cuts, require high-level skills in mediation, conflict resolution, and cultural intervention. Still other crises, such as theft or catastrophe, although they cause significant stress for college leaders, are generally unforeseeable, although colleges need to have policies and procedures in place to handle these if they occur.

SOURCES OF AND POTENTIAL FOR CONFLICT

Sitting presidents have experienced crises and conflict as part of their tenure as chief executive officers and undoubtedly as members of leadership teams in previous assignments. Presidents routinely evaluate and analyze the relatively hostile environments inside and outside of the college in which they operate. Deciding how they will resolve a conflict or crisis is often the first consideration. Typically, the situational leadership and decisional style chosen would largely account for the success or failure of the overall strategy employed.

Research conducted in several environments indicates that crises tend to be better managed by leaders who take charge and exercise more power than they do in routine matters. Furthermore, leaders who act in a confident and decisive manner are usually more effective

(Yukl, 1998, p. 32). Mulder and his associates, in a study of bank managers, found that consultation with the senior and mid-level leadership team was used less in crises than in routine situations and yielded less than satisfactory solutions (Mulder, Ritsema, van Eck, & de Jong, 1970).

Increasing complexity and interdependence in America's community colleges are tremendous sources of conflict for presidents and their leadership teams. The various parties, such as faculty, staff, administration, students, collective bargaining units, and the board, must work out their relationships across the boundaries, between individuals, and among groups. Failure to accomplish this will undoubtedly lead to a college climate that is unproductive, undeserved by the community, and destructive to all concerned. Walton and McKersie (1965) defined the process of conflict resolution as "the deliberate interaction of two or more complex social units which are attempting to define or redefine the terms of their interdependence" (cited in Hampton, Summers, & Webber, 1987, p. 621).

Community colleges, perhaps more than most organizations, are democratic in nature. Individualistic people feel free to pursue their personal interests; honest citizens can disagree on the limits of their freedoms; and when they start bumping into each other, sparks begin to fly (Hampton et al., 1987, p. 620). It is the role of leadership to resolve these conflicts through planning, influencing, structuring, directing, and controlling. When resolving conflict situations, leaders must remember that conflict is inevitable and at some level desirable. When the energy directed in conflict situations is positive and problem solving in nature, effective leaders can steer the enterprise out of the storm and toward smoother water.

The potential for conflict in community colleges depends on how compatible or incompatible are the goals of the parties involved, to what extent the parties share the resources, and how much the parties must work together to get the job done (see Figure 10.1). For

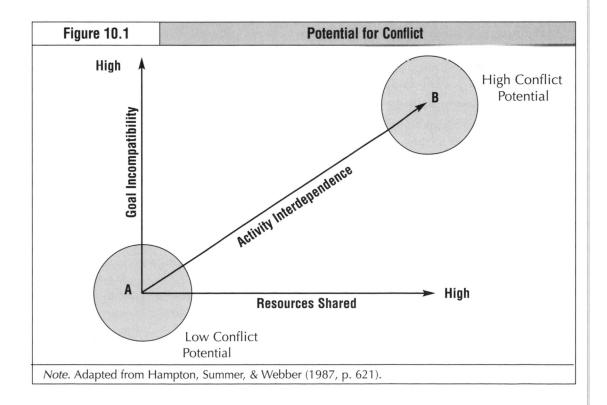

Figure 10.1   **Potential for Conflict**

Note. Adapted from Hampton, Summer, & Webber (1987, p. 621).

example, if two executive deans do not see the goals of student development in the same light, the resources are not adequate for both to accomplish the mission, and they must work together to achieve an important outcome, not only will the two deans be in conflict, but often so will the individuals and units involved. The problem as stated is a classic problem in community colleges, and the solution has often been to place the student development dean under the instructional dean or to combine the two positions into a single administrator.

At the intra-personnel level, the potential for conflict is present with each decision made that affects others in some way. Intra-personnel conflict is a growth industry because everyone wants to participate in decisions that affect them. In our society today, fewer and fewer individuals are willing to accept decisions that affect some aspect of their work or life when they were not in the decision-making loop.

Solving conflict situations requires the ability to identify and deal with the four aspects of conflict: (1) antecedent conditions to an overt struggle (e.g., scarcity of resources); (2) affective states (such as tension or hostility); (3) cognitive states (for example, the perception that someone or some entity acted against the person's interest); and (4) conflicting behavior (ranging from passive resistance to overt aggression) (Hampton et al., 1987, p. 627). Conflict resolution in the community college setting further requires an understanding of the organizational culture. Faculties collectively are relatively predictable in the stakes and stands regarding a specific issue. So are administrators or student services and financial personnel, as well as other groups in the college.

Allison (1971), discussing the Cuban missile crisis, argued that the strongest tool in conflict management and resolution is to employ the old saw, "Where one stands on an issue is dependent on where one sits in the organization." Culture shapes behavior, and subcultures yield rich terrain for conflict to develop.

The resolution of organizational conflict is essential for the establishment of the situational leadership and decisional models presented in this chapter. Training the executive team, including the president, is essential if they are to develop the skills necessary to deal with intra-personal, inter-group, and intra-organization conflict. Organizations such as the Duke University Conflict Resolution Team stand ready to provide necessary training to organizations perceiving the need for such experiences.

Managing Conflict and Avoiding Crises

Some commonly used methods for responding to conflict and avoiding crises are not so much resolution techniques as they are management processes. The most effective of these management techniques are dominance, hierarchical appeal, restructuring, and negotiation.

Dominance

Individual dominance simply means that the strong survive and the weak retreat to fight another day. If one party can dominate the other, as in an athletic contest, the weaker of the two combatants leaves the field. In community colleges, this defeat is symbolic and the individual can be fired or demoted, or may remain as one of the "walking wounded." Although individual dominance often resolves the conflict, it results in a loss for the institution: In essence, it is a failure of leadership. As such, individual dominance is, or should be, a last resort.

The dominance of coalitions is common because of the perception that the larger the group, the more power it can employ to resolve an issue. The constant conflicts among coalitions in the community college can, and often do, lead to full-blown crises. Most often these flash points occur between the faculty and the administration, with the president as the focal point. These conflicts often occur when one coalition believes that another coalition is receiving more resources (pay or budget), and pressure is brought to bear to equalize the desired goal.

Hierarchical Appeal

Conflict can also be resolved by appeal to a higher authority. Here, two individuals or groups in conflict can appeal to a common superior. This process provides a means of making difficult decisions through a judicial or bureaucratic and hierarchical structure. Within the community college, the president, the board, and the executive team have responsibility to make fair and well-reasoned decisions. Community college leaders must understand the right of their followers to due process. The open door of the president is employed only when the conflict has not been resolved at the lower level, and is often the court of last resort. Effective presidents are generally able to see all sides of the issue and, without openly disapproving the decisions of their leadership team, can find ways to resolve the problem that may not have been available to others.

Restructuring

The third conflict resolution technique is restructuring. In community colleges people must work together to achieve the mission assigned by higher authority. To minimize conflict, leaders can design and modify the organizational structure so as to avoid conflict-provoking work patterns. Leaders can merge two units, make two units dependent on one another, create a buffer with a linking position, or even duplicate two units if the workload justifies such a solution. (See Hampton et al., 1987, chapter 11, for further examples of restructuring.)

Negotiation

Probably the most popular techniques for handling differences in organizations such as community colleges are bargaining and negotiation (Atkinson, 1977). Here, we will cover some of the basic concepts involved in these processes. *Bargaining power* refers to another person's inducement to agree to your terms. Simply put, my bargaining power is your cost of disagreeing with my terms relative to your cost of agreeing to my terms (Hampton et al., 1987, p. 624). A classic example is the collective bargaining unit's power to bargain over working conditions, hours, and compensation. In arenas where bargaining units do not exist, the state (public employees' associations) may establish independent relationships between the faculty members or other employees and management of the college.

Distributive bargaining is similar to dominance, but it is done with the recognition that either party can hurt the other, and that both will be around after the bargaining session is completed. Distributive bargaining is similar to a zero-sum game in that what either side gains is at the expense of the other (see Rapoport, 1999). Hence, the issue will come back to the table in future sessions. *Integrative bargaining* occurs when the negotiators are able to reach a solution that enhances both parties and produces high joint benefit (see Atkinson, 1977). Many community colleges have used this technique, which is often called win-win or consensus bargaining. In this type of bargaining, the problems are identified and both sides look together to fine common ground to resolve or address the problems.

Bargaining is not for the faint of heart, nor is it for amateurs. Training is necessary to best represent the organization or the individuals involved. Along with credentials, people successful in bargaining roles often exhibit a combination of cautious trust, indicating a willingness to cooperate, and firmness, preventing partners from exploiting their coopera-tiveness (Hampton et al., 1987, p. 637). When bargaining breaks down, a mediator is often called to action; however, mediators can also be used before a situation escalates.

One type of negotiator is the mediator. Mediators do not decide who is right and who is wrong. They do not even decide what is right (those decisions are for an arbitrator or judge). Mediators simply attempt to stop the spiral of conflict by encouraging each party to acknowledge that they have, in fact, injured the other party, rather than simply to continue to demand each other's surrender. Walton (1967) offered the following advice to mediators, leaders, negotiators, and managers:

- confront and invite differences
- listen with understanding
- do not evaluate
- clarify the nature of the issue
- recognize and accept feelings
- suggest a procedure for resolving differences
- cope with threats to reasonable agreements (cited in Hampton et al., 1987, pp. 637–638).

DECISION MAKING FOR CONFLICT RESOLUTION

Perhaps no set of leadership competencies is more important in the resolution of crisis and conflict than the process of making decisions. In hundreds of climate studies conducted by the National Initiative for Leadership and Institutional Effectiveness (NILIE) at North Carolina State University during the past five years, no single item has been rated less satis-fying than "the extent to which decisions are made at the appropriate level at this institu-tion" (Baker, 2001). Next ranked is a similar item, "the extent to which I participate in decisions at the college." Typically, the rankings for these two items correlate well with a third, "the extent to which a spirit of cooperation exists at this college."

In other words, where staff, faculty, and administrators perceive that decisions are not made at the appropriate level, they feel they are not involved in decisions they believe that they should be helping to resolve. They also may perceive that a spirit of cooperation does not exist at the college. Interesting here is that most do not want to be involved in all deci-sions, but only those that affect their particular roles, jobs, or property rights. Although it is important to get the right people involved in decision making, it is crucial to get the right people involved in finding solutions to crises and conflicts that affect the health and well-being of the college.

Most problems involving crises or interpersonal or organizational conflict are ill-structured. Generally, there is considerable ambiguity and limited information about the problems, and the problems are redefined as new information becomes available. Examples of other situations that were resolved successfully are not available, more than one person is likely to influence the decision process, and the decision process is likely to extend over a long period of time (Ungson, Braunstein, & Hall, 1981). In general, the higher the level where the problem exists, and the further the problem has developed toward crisis, the more likely it is that the president and the leadership team have not previously resolved a similar issue (Simon, 1959, p. 3).

The leader's basic dilemma in dealing with crisis or conflict situations is generally a discrepancy between what is believed to be fair and desirable and what intuition leads one to

Table 10.1	Types of Decision Styles Used to Resolve Conflict				
Descriptor Symbol	Leader Behavior	Locus of Information	Role of the Group	Decision Maker	Goleman's Leadership Style
One-on-One Conflict					
A1	You solve the problem or make the decision	You possess all needed information	—	Leader	Authoritative
A2	You solve the problem or make the decisions. You generate alternatives.	You collect needed information from group. You elect to share problem or not to share problem as appropriate	—	Leader	Authoritative
Group vs. Individual Conflict					
C1	You share problem with appropriate individuals in one-on-one meetings	You collect individual ideas and suggestions. These inputs may or may not influence your decisions.	To individually provide data you need	Leader	Affiliative, coaching
Group vs. Group Conflict—Institutional Crisis					
C2	You share the problem with the group in an open session	You collect individual ideas and suggestions	To collectively provide data you need	Leader	Coaching
G2	You share the problem with the group in open sessions	Together, you and the group generate and evaluate the problem	To collectively solve inputs	Group, with leader	Democratic, coaching
Note. Adapted from Vroom (1973, p. 70).					

decide in actual practice. Understanding the staff, faculty, and administration's desire to be involved in decisions that affect their work lives, as well as their desire to see decisions pushed down to the lowest common denominator, forces the effective leader to be very careful in "deciding how to decide" conflict and crisis situations. It is beyond the scope of this chapter to deal with decision making in general, so this discussion will deal only with crisis and conflict situations.

In analyzing who decides and at what level decisions are resolved, Vroom and Yetton (1973) developed a process for decision making. Their research identified five decisional styles that leaders stated they used in deciding who would resolve an issue (see Table 10.1). There are two versions of the authoritative decision style, two versions of the consultative style, and one version of the group style.

The A1 style is essentially resolved by the leader, is primarily employed in one-on-one interpersonal conflict, and generally has the characteristics of Goleman's "authoritative" leadership style (discussed in the next section). The A2 style involves the leader's structure and the generation of possible solutions. Like A1, A2 is generally employed in one-on-one conflict and generally has the characteristics of Goleman's authoritative style. Using the C1 style, the leader shares the problem, one on one, with involved individuals, or in individual versus group conflict, and employs Goleman's "affiliative" and "coaching" styles. Using the C2 decisional style, the leader shares and solves the problem with the appropriate group in open session. C2 is generally employed in a group verses group conflict or institutional crises, and the leader typically makes use of a combination of authoritative and coaching styles. The G2 style is like the C2 style except that once the problem is structured (i.e., the problem has been stated, and alternatives have been generated together), the leader does not attempt to move the group toward a particular outcome. The research shows that under these circumstances the group is much more likely to generate effective solutions than if these solutions were decided by the leader and provided to them. This style employs democratic and coaching styles and is most effective in large group-to-group conflicts and major organizational crises.

Vroom and Yetton's rules to protect decisional quality and to ensure acceptance of the decision by the followers are illustrated in Table 10.2. The information rule states that if the leader does not possess sufficient information, then the leader must not use A1. If time is of the essence, A2 or C1 can be employed. If not, and the leader desires to use the situation for team building, then C2 or G2 can be used. The goal congruence rule states that when quality is an issue, and when followers are in conflict regarding the goals to be achieved, then G2 cannot be used. Again, if time is of the essence, the A1 or A2 decisional styles can be used; if team building is desired, the C1 or C2 styles can be used.

The routine problem rule states that when outcome quality is an issue, when the leader does not possess sufficient information necessary to make a decision, and when the problem is new to the problem solvers, then A1, A2, and C1 must not be used. This situation precludes a timely solution and requires a C2 or G2 style. The acceptance rule states that when acceptance by followers is critical, and it cannot be predicted whether or not the decision will be accepted, and when a crisis must be avoided, autocratic decisional styles cannot be used. Again C1, C2, or G2 decisional styles must be used. The conflict rule states that when acceptance of the decision is critical, a crisis is likely, and followers are likely to be in conflict or disagreement over the appropriate solution, A1, A2, or G2 cannot be used. In this case only C1 or C2 has a high probability for success. The fairness rule states that when a quality outcome is not important, but acceptance by the group is critical, only G2 is recommended. The acceptance priority rule states that if acceptance of the decision is critical to avoid a crisis and followers can be trusted to forego the benefits to themselves for the good of the college, then G2 is the only feasible alternative.

Much water has passed under the bridge since the development of the Vroom and Yetton model in 1973. At that time, leaders who used the model appropriately were success-

Table 10.2	Seven Rules to Protect Quality and Ensure Acceptance of Decisions
Decision-Making Rules	**Description and Decision Styles to Consider**
1. The Information Rule	When the quality of the decision is important and when you do not possess sufficient information or expertise to make the decision yourself, A1 is not a feasible behavior. **Consider A2, C1, C2, G2**
2. The Goal Congruence Rule	When the quality of the decision is important and when followers do not see payoffs for themselves in the problem situation, G2 is not a feasible behavior. **Consider A1, A2, C1, C2**
3. The Routine Problem Rule	When the quality of the decision is important, when you do not possess sufficient information or expertise to make the decision yourself, and if the problem is not routine, A1, A2, and C1 are not feasible behaviors. **Consider C2 or G2**
4. The Acceptance Rule	When the acceptance of the decision by followers is critical to effective implementation, and you cannot predict accurately whether or not your decision will be accepted, A1 and A2 are not feasible behaviors. **Consider C1, C2, or G2**
5. The Conflict Rule	When the acceptance of the decision is critical, autocratic decisions unacceptable, and followers are likely to be in conflict or disagreement over the appropriate solution, A1, A2, and C1 are not feasible behaviors. **Consider C2 or G2**
6. The Fairness Rule	When the quality of the decision is not important and when acceptance is critical, A1, A2, C1, and C2 are not feasible behaviors. **Consider G2**
7. The Acceptance Priority Rule	When the acceptance of the decision is critical and followers can be trusted to forgo benefits to themselves for the good of the organization, A1, A2, C1, and C2 are not feasible behaviors. **Consider G2**

Note. Adapted from Vroom (1973, p. 70).

ful only 65% of the time. The idea of appropriate leadership styles similar to Goleman's framework should have had the net effect of raising the percentage considerably. In some situations of high stress, a lack of trust, and a history of poor crisis management, it is likely that no solution will return an institution to a climate of trust and productivity. At this time a leadership change is probably necessary.

LEADERSHIP STYLES AND CONFLICT RESOLUTION

The first recommendation to college presidents who are facing a crisis where little compromise is possible is that it is best for the leader to be directive, goal-oriented, and decisive. This does not mean that the president should not consult team members possessing special expertise. However, in the face of crises of resources, confidence will undoubtedly be the best course of action in the long run. Goleman's (2000) research supports the conclusion that in crises the authoritative leadership style has the best chance of finding a resolution. He described the authoritative style as follows:

- Mobilizes people toward a vision
- Communicates to follows, "Join me in resolving this issue"
- Creates confidence, empathy, and a change orientation among followers
- Works best when change requires a new vision
- Works best when clear direction is needed
- Creates the most powerful impact on college climate. (Goleman, 2000, p. 82)

    Goleman (2000) described what leaders do. He believes that although leaders set strategy, motivate followers, create the mission, model the values, and build culture, but that most

Table 10.3	Four Critical Leadership Styles			
	Authoritative	**Affiliative**	**Democratic**	**Coaching**
Leader's Preference	Demands compliance with policy	Mobilizes people toward vision	Acts collaboratively, builds emotional bonds	Develops the team for the future
The Style	"Let's get it done"	"Come with me"	"People come first"	"Let's try this"
Emotional Intelligence	Self-confidence, Empathy	Empathy, Communication	Collaboration, Team Building	Development of others' self-awareness
Best Time	Changes require a new vision	To resolve crises among people, units	To build a consensus	To help improve performance
Impact on Climate	Powerfully positive	Positive	Positive	Positive

Note. Coercive and pacesetting styles are not discussed because of their negative effects on climate. These should be reserved for situations where other styles have proven ineffective in one-on-one situations. Adapted from Goleman (2000).

of all they should get results. The results that he speaks of cannot be gained when the college is crippled with conflict and when crises sweep in like crashing waves from a hurricane. Goleman's most powerful styles are identified and described in Table 10.3.

Goleman believes that the authoritative style should be backed up with two additional styles in crises. Effective leaders will also employ the affiliative and the coaching styles. The affiliative style creates harmony and builds emotional bonds, creates an environment where people come first in resolving the crisis, builds empathy and teamwork, and increases communication flow. The affiliative style can heal rifts within a team and can motivate people in stressful circumstances. Its effect on aspects of climate such as flexibility, responsibility, standards, rewards, clarity, and commitment are positive.

The coaching style serves to create leaders who will be able to resolve future crises, offers new approaches for new problems, is oriented toward developing followers, and provides empathy for the team and self-awareness of their importance to the college. The coaching style helps team members improve their own effectiveness at their particular level in the organization and develops long-term, problem-solving competencies. Its effect on the organizational climate is similar to that of the affiliative style (Goleman, 2000, pp. 80–83).

One might ask why these styles do not work under all circumstances and situations. Many studies, including Goleman's and others, support the idea that the more styles a leader exhibits, the better his or her chance of resolving problems and challenges of all types. Leaders who have mastered four or more of the styles—especially the authoritative, democratic, affiliative, and coaching—achieve the very best performance in routine or crisis situations. (See Goleman, 2000, for a full discussion of his concepts.)

An excellent team-building exercise for the president's leadership team would be to develop scenarios and case studies involving crisis and conflict situations that have occurred at other colleges, and then to resolve these issues employing Goleman's model or others. If climate studies or other information have been gathered, the team can also work on crises that are likely to happen in the particular environment of the college. In addition to the leadership style of the president and the executive team, the processes of problem solving and decision making are also important tools in the hand of an effective leader.

LEADERSHIP AND RESPONSIBILITY

Crises typically are not born of the leaders' direct involvement. They can be external or internal. External crises are often the result of political infighting for resources, power, or values. Crises of resource allocation often leave little room to maneuver. Internal crises often involve issues that have been brewing for a long period of time. Occasionally, the president may be a chief causal factor. If the president believes himself or herself to be unable to live with external crisis of the nature just described, he or she should be willing to resign to demonstrate the unwillingness to live with a moral dilemma. If the president finds that he or she is at the center of an internal crisis that was primarily caused by a failure of leadership, of personality issues, or of moral conviction, serious self-evaluation, with or without coaching, should be the order of the day. Repeated failures in this regard should be grounds for breaking out and updating one's resume or considering other options.

Conflict permeates every aspect of our lives. Holton (1995) noted that conflict is inevitable in higher education, where academic freedom is revered and free thinking is encouraged. Leaders typically react defensively to conflict and often fail to take into account the fundamental and necessary role that conflict plays in preserving the existing culture within the college. Community college presidents must realize that conflict, although anxiety-provoking, does not necessarily indicate a breakdown of the existing culture or a failure of leadership (Hampton et al., 1987, p. 620).

It is the responsibility of the senior leadership team under the direction of the president to identify, acknowledge, and eventually resolve conflict with a minimum of organizational turmoil and hostility among combatants. In order to achieve these ends, the senior leadership team should be trained in conflict resolution tactics and in creative problem-solving techniques (Baker, 1992).

Conclusion

This chapter provides an overview of successful crisis management in the community college. Our essential position is that crises, whether generated in the environment outside the college or as the extension of conflict among individuals or between units or organizations, hinders effective leadership and hurts colleges that are attempting to serve their citizens and the community. Crises brought on by factors in the larger communities and systems, such as budget cuts, are inevitable and most often nonnegotiable. However, the effective management of conflict inside the college is the prerequisite to an effective organization. Presidents must give high priority to building a strong, mutually supporting organization because the inability to manage an external crisis—because an internal crisis takes up the energy necessary to fight and win—often is the first step in organizational decline. It is then that leadership changes are certain to follow.

References

Allison, G. (1971). *Essence of decision: Explaining the Cuban missile crisis.* Boston: Little, Brown.

Atkinson, G. G. M. (1977). *The effective negotiator: A practical guide to the strategies and tactics of conflict bargaining* (2nd ed.). London: Quest Research Publications.

Baker, G. A., III., & Associates (Eds.). (1992). *Cultural leadership: Inside America's community colleges.* Washington, DC: Community College Press.

Baker, G. A., III. (2001). *The Pace report.* Raleigh: North Carolina State University, National Initiative for Leadership and Institutional Effectiveness.

Goleman, D. 2000. Leadership that gets results. *Harvard Business Review, 78*(2), 78–90.

Hampton, D., Summers, C., & Webber, R. (1987). *Organizational behavior and the practice of management.* New York: Harper Collins.

Holton, S. (1995). *New directions in higher education: Conflict management in higher education.* San Francisco: Jossey-Bass.

Mulder, M., Ritsema, J., van Eck, J., & de Jong, R. (1970). An organization in crisis and crisis conditions. *Human Relations, 24,* 19–41.

Rapoport, A. (1999). *Two-person game theory.* Mineola, NY: Dover Publications.

Simon, H. (1959). Theories of decision making in economics and behavioral science. *American Economic Review, 49,* 253–283.

Ungson, G., Braunstein, D., & Hall, P. (1981). Managerial information processing: A research review. *Administrative Science Quarterly, 26,* 116–134.

Vroom, V. H. (1973, Spring). A new look at managerial decision making. *Organizational Dynamics.*

Vroom, V., & Yetton, P. (1973). *Leadership and decision making.* Pittsburgh: University of Pittsburgh Press.

Walton, R. E. (1967). Third-party rules in interdepartmental conflict. *Industrial Relations, 7*(1), 29.

Walton, R., & McKersie, R. (1965). *A behavioral theory of labor negotiations: An analysis of a social system.* New York: McGraw-Hill.

Yukl, G. (1998). *Leadership in organizations* (4th ed.). Saddle River, NJ: Prentice Hall.

Chapter 11

FIRST-YEAR STRATEGIES FOR NEW PRESIDENTS

Tony Zeiss

Real excellence and humility are not incompatible . . . on the contrary, they are twin sisters.

—Jean Baptiste Lacordaire (cited in Murphy, 1978)

Aspiring community college presidents generally have worked about 25 years in their field, have earned a terminal degree, and have changed colleges two or three times to obtain the experience needed to even be considered for the position. Yet, believe it or not, the average community college president holds the office for only about five years! Why, then, do people aspire to hold such a tenuous position? They seek a presidency because of the opportunities that the position provides for making a difference in the lives of others and in their communities. They seek to be among those leaders whose institutions enroll approximately 10 million students in credit and noncredit courses each year. Indeed, serving as a community college president is a worthy endeavor, recognized by policymakers, opinion leaders, and communities. As Vaughn wrote, "Community college presidents help to chart the educational, social, and economic life of thousands of communities across the nation" (1986).

In this chapter I present an overview of the challenges faced by new community college presidents that have been addressed in some form throughout this book. It is specifically written, however, as a guideline, synthesizing the many approaches to developing leading strategies, as presented by the authors.

ESSENTIAL PRINCIPLES FOR NEW PRESIDENTS

Being selected as the CEO of a community college is a wonderful career achievement. However, the presidency is not something just to be achieved; it must become a way of life. Once individuals assume the responsibilities and the opportunities of the presidency, they and their families become forever changed in many ways. Effective presidents, for example, cease to be as private, independent, or self-determined as they once were. Great presidents and, often, their spouses, become focused on others almost 24 hours each day.

To be effective, college presidents must constantly remind themselves of what we believe are essential principles of leadership. Some of these may appear simplistic compared with many of the strategies and ideas presented in earlier chapters, and so they are. Yet simple does not necessarily mean easy. Each of the authors of this book has experienced the difficulty of striving to embody these principles on a day-to-day basis.

Commit to excellence. The decision to apply for a position as a community college president is a big one that takes aspiration, confidence, and a whole lot of thought about how the job of president will affect one's life. To be chosen for the position is an honor that gives rise to feelings from joy to fear to even a bit of bravado. However, as any incumbent or ex-college president will tell you, success comes not when you get the job of president, but some time after, when you have demonstrated that you can do the job well. The faster one can grasp this and commit to getting the job done well, the better the chances for survival and for becoming a respected college and community leader.

Lead from a personal vision, mission, and set of values. Leaders like to talk about the importance of having clear, shared visions, missions, and values for colleges, but having a personal vision, mission, and set of values is equally important for college presidents. A CEO who has an unclear vision or mission will soon have no one following. But a vision is not enough; a leader must also have a solid set of values. Great leaders are anchored in truth and recognize moral authority. A leader whose set of values is fragile will fail regardless of the clarity of his or her vision and mission.

Develop a passion for the job. The primary difference between good college CEOs and great ones is not leadership style, charisma, or intelligence. Truly great presidents have a passion for what they do and whom they serve. Passion persuades, enthusiasm excites, and others always respect sincerity of purpose.

Lead for results. Popular leaders are always appreciated, but the truly appreciated leaders do far more than build good relationships. In the final analysis, key stakeholders of the college, board members, financial contributors, policymakers, community leaders, and faculty judge a president by his or her ability to make things happen.

Be honest. Dishonesty will get a president dismissed faster than a speeding bullet. Mature leaders understand that it is far more important to tell the truth, all of it, than to protect an ego or reputation by stretching or limiting the truth. Once a president's integrity is in question, the end is in sight. Hold onto your integrity as you would to a lifeline.

Be fair and respectful. People the world over have a keen sense of fairness. This intuitive notion intensifies in the workplace. Smart presidents recognize the importance of treating all people with fairness and respect. Employees who perceive inequity or disrespect will rebel overtly, or worse, covertly.

Be humble. Confidence is respected and admired, but humility is required of college presidents. In the collegiate environment, presidents are expected to lead with confidence and optimism, but in a humble fashion. Successful presidents regularly remind themselves that they serve at the pleasure of the community, the faculty and staff, the students, and the board of trustees.

Be adaptable. Being able to adapt has kept some plant and animal species alive for eons while others perished in changing conditions. Serving as a president is similar to living in nature, things are always changing. Being able to anticipate and adapt to change is essential for presidents.

Know your business. Successful presidents are people of substance, and they know their business. More important, they recognize their weak areas and take action to eliminate them. New presidents should assess their strengths and weaknesses in each area of college operations and strategize to learn what they need to be able to lead effectively. Having good people supporting leaders is essential for success, but having the knowledge base to lead and operate the organization is equally important.

Delegate, but monitor. Effective leaders understand that their employees drive the success of the college. Without productive employees, nothing can be accomplished or achieved. Although good leaders resist telling employees how to achieve some goal, they do exercise judicious follow-through to ensure that the goal is being pursued and will be accomplished. Delegation without follow-through is a prescription for failure.

Do sweat the small stuff. It is not generally the grand activities of the college that impede progress—it is the small things that are usually most disruptive. Employee complaints, audit exceptions, an accreditation recommendation, an indiscreet public remark, a missed funeral, a glass of wine left on an expense voucher, or the perception that the president does not have time for people—all are very important issues, however small they may seem at the time.

Accept criticism, share the glory. In difficult times, effective leaders accept the criticism of the organizations they lead. In good times, effective presidents credit their faculty and staff for the accomplishments of the college.

BUILD TRUSTING RELATIONSHIPS

New presidents sometimes have the mistaken idea that they are finally in control and that their ideas will take root and drive the college. However, veteran presidents know that the first year in office is a time for building relationships, not changing fundamental elements of the college. There are exceptions, of course. For example, if the board of trustees hires the president to make immediate changes, then the president will have to be especially skillful in building relationships quickly. Veteran presidents also recognize that a president's power is largely illusory. They accept responsibility for the college, but they realize that major decisions and directions for the organization must be collegial and collaborative in nature.

The role of a community college president has expanded from leading college communities in defining their vision, mission, and values to emphasizing fundraising, legislative efforts, and business relationships. Building and keeping a strong image of the college requires working with more constituent groups than before. These expanding demands make the ability to persuade, collaborate, and sell paramount for success. The ability to influence others is a key characteristic of leaders and deserves special attention by new presidents.

Presidents continually struggle with the question of how they can provide strong leadership without alienating their faculty, board, students, and policymakers (Vaughn, 1986). Sometimes these interest groups hold strong and opposing views about how the college should operate. Other times, presidents will receive widespread support of their efforts. Experienced presidents learn to build solid relationships with each college stakeholder group in order to stay abreast of the ideas and issues important to each. In this way, the president can gain a better sense of when and to whom to delegate or direct. By simultaneously working to reconcile differences while upholding the vision, mission, and values of the institution, college presidents can develop and maintain trusting relationships. The most important step in building trusting relationships is to take time to identify whom you should get to know (and in what order) even before you take over the position. Key college stakeholders are as follows.

- *Board members.* Get to know each board member and his or her spouse individually, as it is critical that new presidents thoroughly understand the expectations, points of view, and the vision of the board members. A misunderstanding at this level is a good prescription for failure.
- *Administrators and faculty.* Meeting with key administrators and faculty is a top priority. Next, make appointments with faculty leaders on their turf or at a coffee shop. Be sure to get help with this, as the pecking order among faculty is very real, and woe to the president who visits those on the lower rung before visiting those in the upper order.
- *Funding sources.* Consider who funds the college. If it is the legislature, become friends with your delegation as soon as possible. Invite them to the college. If it is the county commission or if your college is a taxing authority, get to know the commissioners and community leaders.
- *Staff and student leaders.* College staff members are very important to any team, and getting to know your student leadership is essential.
- *The college foundation.* The college foundation will be an important resource for achieving certain aspects of your fundraising and program development goals. Take the time to get to know the foundation's staff and board members, and to understand the foundation's own strategic goals and objectives.
- *Business leaders.* Harvard professor James Austin's (1999) research demonstrates the level of influence business leaders exert in their communities. It is this "invisible leadership" group that presidents must also learn to court. Many presidents have survived internal problems because of external support, and the reverse. Effective presidents must quickly build support for the college and for themselves from all who have influence on the college.

Former governor Roy Romer of Colorado understood the importance of relationships as a preeminent leadership tool. Romer had excellent interpersonal skills and knew how to make others like him and help him with state issues. He employed two techniques: He focused on the individuals he was talking to as if they were the most important people in the room, and he constantly asked others, "How are we doing?" Think about any good leader, and you will find that he or she employs these same two techniques. A strong and sincere focus on individuals and continuous affirmation will help build great relationships.

LEAD FOR SUCCESS

Effective leadership styles are those that work for both the leader and the organization being led. Whatever style they use, community college presidents should remember to be themselves and acknowledge the situational nature of leadership.

Peter Drucker (1999) outlined his mentors' leadership lessons and discussed five primary leadership lessons he learned from three of his early bosses. The lessons evidently helped him, and most apply to first-year college presidents:

1. Treat people differently, based on their strengths.
2. Set high standards, but give people the freedom and responsibility to do their jobs.
3. Performance reviews must be honest, exacting, and an integral part of the job.
4. People learn most when teaching others.
5. Effective leaders earn respect, but do not have to be liked.

It is useful to read the advice of respected leaders like Drucker, but what works well for one leader may not work as well for another. For example, leaders do not have to be liked, but they are generally much more effective if they are. Decide what leadership techniques work for you, and be true to them. No one can emulate how other people lead if it does not come naturally or sincerely. If you try to be something you are not, your behavior will be inconsistent and confuse employees. Assess what works, determine what principles you will follow, and apply them as situations dictate.

The ability to apply policies in situational context without violating those principles is important. For example, recently some of my employees had extended illnesses and had run out of sick days and vacation leave. We could not violate state policy, but we established a method for employees to give their accumulated sick days to those who needed them. Leaders must hold fast to the college's policies but apply them in a fair and contextual manner. At the end of their tenure, presidents are remembered for their compassion for and confidence in their employees, not for their unbendable rules and regulations. Wise presidents quickly determine what is most important, and they communicate this continuously.

When I became president of one college, it was important to establish what I was about and what the board expected of the organization. In my first address to the faculty and staff, I encouraged them to consider two questions before making any decision regarding curriculum, procedures, or services: Is it good for our students? Is it good for our community? Ten years later, I still encourage them to ask these questions. This mental exercise forces our college to focus on our constituents rather than ourselves. Keeping the focus on customers is an effective hedge against complacency and arrogance.

New presidents also face a leadership challenge with their key officers or cabinet members. It is essential that cabinet members know what is expected of them and feel that they are part of a team. Once the new president has received clear direction from the trustees, he or she should hold a cabinet retreat away from the college. The purpose should be to build trusting relationships, establish a common vision, and communicate expectations. Astute presidents will verbally recognize the strengths of each cabinet member and will help establish a strong sense of involvement with all leadership team members. A weekly cabinet meeting generally keeps the leadership team well informed.

Employees must also understand the college's vision and know what is important to the president. Effective presidents are consistent in their messages and their behavior. Instructional quality, adequate resources, fiscal integrity, and a positive image for the organization are the four most important presidential concerns. Presidents should take advantage of each opportunity to communicate the importance of these fundamental tenets to their employees.

BE PREPARED TO DEAL WITH CHANGE

Colleges evolve through life cycles. There is the excitement of the birth of the college, followed by growth and adolescence when the organization is determining what it should become. After about 15 years, the college begins to mature, and somewhere around 30 years, decline will begin. Good leadership is required during all of these stages, but dealing with the declining period can be especially challenging.

The best way to stop decline is by intervening with a comprehensive strategic planning process that involves every member of the college culture in order to gain college-wide support for a shift in strategic direction. The planning process must involve the examination of external environments. It must be backed by the organization's will to adjust the college's vision, mission, and programs to head in whatever direction is articulated. This is not an easy process, especially when dealing with long-tenured faculty and staff, but it is being done successfully in many places.

For example, Fox Valley Technical College in Appleton, Wisconsin, and Lamar Community College in Lamar, Colorado, embraced the concept of Total Quality Management in the early 1990s and transformed themselves into organizations that seek continuous improvement. Central Piedmont Community College in Charlotte, North Carolina, and Sinclair Community College in Dayton, Ohio, have made the transition from teacher- and teaching-focused colleges to learner- and learning-focused colleges over the past four years.

Some valuable research on change has been conducted in the past few years. The American Council on Education recently published a monograph on change with respect to presidents and governing boards. This research revealed that boards and presidents successful with dealing with change

- Approached change collaboratively
- Were intentional in their actions
- Were reflective about their change endeavors
- Learned from their actions and adjusted their plans

In effect, good leaders will create learning organizations that have the capacity for continuous change (Hill, Green, & Eckel, 2001).

In an excellent handbook on dealing with the stress of change, experts on change management Pritchett and Pound (2001) offered the sound, practical advice to put you in charge of managing the pressure of change. Neither the organization nor other people are likely to be able to lighten your psychological load. The following formula is an effective model for leading change:

- Build trusting relationships
- Create anxiety by demonstrating the need for change
- Paint a clear vision to satisfy the need
- Connect change to the organization's core values
- Tie change to the strength and pride of the organization
- Use reward systems that work
- Communicate clearly and often
- Arouse passion
- Be consistent

Each member of the college helps to shape the college's culture. How employees perceive the purpose of the college and their contribution to that purpose is the basis for the institution's climate and culture. Any change that affects their perceptions of purpose and their role as members of the college community is generally seen as threatening or at least disturbing. Most people want to be part of something that allows them to be good contributors to worthy causes, and they need recognition to affirm success in their endeavors. Unfortunately, when we become good at something and continue for several years, we are often deluded into thinking that we are still making a great contribution even if the needs of those we serve have shifted dramatically.

For example, most community colleges have 50% or more of their students attending classes at night and on weekends, yet the majority of services are available only in the daytime. Asking half of a college's employees to work from 1 p.m. to 9 p.m. is likely to be met with resistance. But if the leadership of the college can create some anxiety to drive the need for the change, employees will more readily accept the change, especially if it reinforces their perception of worth.

Tying change to core values of the college is essential for gaining employees' acceptance. For instance, change can be tied to innovation, quality, or service. If your college prides itself on serving the community, the desired change should be clearly positioned as yet another opportunity to serve the community. Offering compressed degrees or self-paced, open-entry courses can be easily tied to this core value. If your college embraces innovation as a core value, any needed change, such as new credentialing via skill certifications, can clearly be proposed as innovative.

To feel real ownership of a change, employees must become passionate about it. Passion is often innate in education professionals, but sometimes they have to see that their leaders have the same passion. Enthusiasm begets enthusiasm, cheerfulness begets cheerfulness, and passion for serving yields passionate service. Presidents have to be the first to become passionate about change.

Sometimes this is not easy to do. A budget reduction is seldom pleasing. However, budget pruning often yields greater efficiencies and forces the closing of programs and services that should have been closed years ago. Budget cuts also provide a common adversary that often strengthens the college community. In this respect, it is important that leaders become passionate about increasing revenue while calling for more efficiency. Smart presidents use adversity as a rallying call for change. When serious adversity occurs, there exist actions that are often useful in galvanizing employees and establishing a strategy to weather the storm. For example, when our college recently faced critical budget cuts and had to cancel hundreds of classes, we employed this list of actions with great success:

- Engage in dialogue with, and seek the advice of, the governing board, foundation board, and advisory boards (we began a new capital campaign that opened with a $5 million gift).
- Engage in dialogue with, and seek the advice of, the college community (we received scores of good ideas for becoming more efficient via e-mail from faculty and staff).
- Establish a clear strategy for becoming more efficient and for increasing resources.
- Engage in dialogue with the editorial boards of local newspapers about the problem and your plan for addressing it.
- Speak about your plan at every opportunity.
- Praise everyone who helps with the plan: instructors who increase class sizes, administrators who teach for free, board members who help with fundraising, and so forth.

Community colleges today face myriad changes. Among these are the growing need to teach and certify occupational skills at nontraditional times and places. Associate in applied science degrees are less and less desired by students, but the demand for community colleges to provide applied baccalaureate degrees is increasing. Traditional methods of serving students are becoming archaic, the demographics of students are changing rapidly, and colleges must become more focused on learning and learners than on tradition. Change will be a constant companion of community colleges in years to come.

Effective leaders must build cultures that are adaptable and receptive to change. The most successful colleges celebrate the core value of service to students and their communities. Once this external focus becomes part of the culture, effecting change becomes part of the college's climate. Colleges that have become self-focused will have a difficult, if not impossible, time with the changes they face. At a recent meeting of the Board of Directors of the American Association of Community Colleges, current chair Jess Carreon identified this important principle by stating: "Communities are defined by jobs and families, not degrees. It's about communities, not colleges." An essay on the future of America's colleges and universities, published by the Knight Higher Education Collaborative, emphasized the need to be more community relevant. "Ultimately, it is the cross-fertilization, the brushing between academy and society that will generate productive energy in both settings" (Knight, 2001). New presidents will do well to quickly assess the climate of their colleges and develop strategic plans for successfully leading their institutions to meet the ever-changing needs of the communities they serve.

Conducting a SWOT analysis, as was described in chapter 2, can be a very useful exercise for new and veteran presidents. This exercise involves a focus group of key college leaders to examine the strengths, weaknesses, opportunities, and threats of the organization. Another quick technique for assessing the interests of the college is to ask employees, students, and employers to list the most important things the college should stop doing, continue doing, and start doing. In any event, ask questions of everyone and listen to the answers.

STRATEGIES FOR SUCCESS

Attract, Develop, and Retain Great Employees

This topic is so important it should become a monograph of its own. At the end of the day, people and their productivity are what make the college succeed or fail. In chapter 8 Simone presented some strategies for staff and faculty development. Here, because of the topic's central importance to the success of community college presidents, I offer some additional strategies.

There is no perfect recruiting formula for all organizations, but many colleges are enjoying successful recruiting because they have taken the responsibility to focus on solutions rather than on the problem. These colleges establish great reputations for supporting their employees, establish a worker supply chain, and provide competitive incentives.

How do colleges develop a good reputation for supporting employees? Simply by listening to them and assisting them whenever and wherever possible. If a college wants a culture where productivity soars, it must treat its employees with the same degree of sincerity and support it uses for its customers. Existing employees will spread the college's reputation as a great place to work.

Developing a worker supply chain is a relatively new phenomenon in the business world. The most successful efforts have been made by those businesses that partner with local workforce preparation programs, high schools, community colleges, technical colleges, and universities. Providing scholarships, internships, cooperative education opportunities, and assisting with program advisory committees are effective methods for establishing a ready supply of emerging workers. I know one CEO who actually enrolls in construction classes at our community college in order to recruit the best students in the class. This seems a bit extreme, but it has been most effective for him. Do not overlook the unemployed, underemployed, immigrants, and senior citizens, many of whom still want meaningful work. Creating connections with these populations can pay big dividends. If these techniques are working for business, they should also work for colleges. Recruiting faculty is more difficult, but growing your own by staying in contact with promising graduates works well.

There are three keys to developing peak performers: training, motivating, and supporting. Training connects directly with productivity. One national study in the early 1990s showed a 300% return on investment for employee training. Yet many businesses fail to recognize the importance of continued training for their employees. Another common mistake is to train the managers, but not the conventional workers. Smart colleges are training all employees. A recent federal government report titled *21st Century Skills for 21st Century Jobs* (Stuart, 1999) indicated that a 10% higher investment in capital equipment yields a 3.4% productivity increase, whereas a 10% increase in training yields an 8.6% productivity increase. People drive our organizations, and a program of continuous learning is essential to success.

Motivating employees is relatively simple once college leaders understand what motivates people. Leaders will do well to remember that recognition, a sense of belonging, and fair compensation are the greatest motivators. People are gregarious beings and have an innate desire to be valued by others. Recognition comes in many forms and is always appreciated if it is deserved and if it is sincere. Superficial recognition is worse than no recognition. To hear "Nice work!" is good, but a mention in the college newsletter is better. The important thing is to remember that those whom we supervise want to be valued and recognized for their contributions. Never miss an opportunity to praise, especially in public.

As social beings, most people love to be part of a group. Indeed, a major part of human identity rests with a sense of belonging, whether to a family, church, or work team. Most people aspire to a real sense of purpose, a sense of significance. Employees seek to be involved in something important, something larger than themselves. Smart leaders will capitalize on this aspect of human nature and will work hard to make all employees feel like part of the team.

Fair compensation is essential for attracting, developing, and retaining peak performers. These days "fair" means much more than just a salary. Flex-time, child care, merit pay, and other incentives have become the norm in many colleges. At a minimum, colleges must offer comprehensive health care and dental care as a standard part of the compensation package and provide opportunities for tax-sheltered investing and wage improvement.

The most effective motivation technique is to reward people for doing good things. Positive reinforcement yields positive results in people. Negative reinforcement yields negative results. If you want positive and productive employees, treat them as positive and productive employees.

Supporting employees also includes investing in their futures. Today's workers want to know if they will have career growth opportunities. It is up to leaders to provide those professional development activities through training, conferences, and seminars that keep them growing.

The importance of retaining peak performers is as critical as ever. There are some effective strategies that management can implement to reduce employee attrition and increase productivity at the same time. The first step toward retaining good employees is to review the college's recruitment process to be sure it is attracting the best candidates possible. The next step is to train employees properly and treat them as valuable members of the team. But to really understand how to keep good employees, one must understand why they leave jobs.

There are many reasons why people leave jobs, and some reasons are simply not preventable. Most job separations, however, can be prevented. If a person believes there is a serious deficiency in any of the fundamental elements of leadership—for example, lack of integrity, lack of recognition, or no sense of value—he or she will be looking for another job. Here are some of the most common reasons why people leave their jobs:

- Distrust
- No recognition
- No sense of purpose
- Poor compensation
- Poor environment
- Insecurity
- Feeling undervalued

When someone leaves a company, management usually speculates about why they left but never bothers to ask the employee. If you want to stop pain, the cause has to be determined. When someone leaves, it is a good idea to hold an exit interview conducted by someone the employee trusts. It is surprising how enlightening such interviews can be. If productivity or morale is down, candid focus group discussions can be helpful in identifying the problem. Employees should be asked for ideas on how to improve productivity or morale. Their responses will be illuminating. The best idea is to hold regular meetings of this type before people leave the college or have problems with productivity or morale.

Cultivate Personal Attributes and Skills that Promote Success

Vaughn's (1986) research identified personal attributes of and skills demonstrated by top community college presidents. Personal attributes that were rated highest in importance are these:

- Integrity
- Judgment
- Courage
- Concern
- Flexibility
- Philosophy
- Loyalty
- Energy level
- Optimism

New presidents will do well to assess themselves honestly with regard to these attributes. Skills and abilities that were ranked highest in importance are the following:

- Producing results
- Selecting people
- Resolving conflicts
- Communicating
- Motivating others
- Analyzing and evaluating
- Defining problems and solutions
- Taking risks
- Delegating
- Being a team member
- Knowing the community

The ability to raise money and to build political and business relationships should be added to this list. The role of community college presidents is changing as the demand for additional operating revenues outstrips public support. Indeed, most colleges now have very active foundations, and many are raising extra money through auxiliary services and through self-supporting classes. Some have even established fee-for-service organizations that are allowed to compete in the private sector. These entrepreneurial organizations have been designed to allow colleges to raise income beyond the usual sources of tuition, millages, and legislative appropriations. New presidents should hone their sales skills because they will need them to be successful.

Desjardins, executive director of the National Institute for Leadership Development, and Huff wrote an excellent book that outlined the competencies for community college leaders in the new millennium (Desjardins & Huff, 2001). This work divides the 22 core competencies of leaders into four major categories: leadership fundamentals, culture and climate, influence, and business management. The authors emphasized the importance of fundraising, globalization, and the changing business culture. It is the most timely and definitive work of its kind and is highly recommended as an additional information source.

Balance Your Life

College presidents have special challenges created by the demands of the job and their own expectations. Presidents have multiple constituents to keep informed and happy: students, parents, trustees, faculty, policymakers, administrators, staff, donors, and the community at large. This is a serious responsibility, and one that demands a great deal of time and thought. Most presidents feel they seldom have any time off. Most successful presidents also place very high demands on themselves, feeling that they must set the standard for achievement. The combination of these external and internal forces tilts the balance of life toward the workplace and mental activity. Finding time for the spiritual and physical dimensions of life often becomes a challenge.

Striking a balance with these three dimensions can be accomplished with some spiritual, mental, and physical discipline. The spiritual dimension is the foundation for the way we see the world, the way we think, and the way we behave. Regardless of one's religious background or beliefs, without a strong spiritual foundation, we would be like ships without rudders, buffeted by every wild wind, never getting to port. The mental dimension is critical for thinking through the decisions of each day. Learn to think about what you think about. Our thoughts become actions that determine what kind of person we become. Yet all of the spiritual grounding and mental alertness in the world is useless unless we possess the physical health to put them to use. Sharpening your mental preparedness, spiritual growth, and physical fitness should become habitual to presidents who hope to have long and successful lives.

Successful presidents should also take time to balance their career lives with their family and personal lives. This is much easier to write about than to accomplish. Most successful presidents give all their energy to their jobs. In the fast-paced, ever-changing environment of the presidency, it is easy to neglect your loved ones and yourself. In the long run, however, people seldom remember self-made martyrs. These jobs can and will kill you if you let them. Do not let it happen to you as it has to many over the years! Spend meaningful time with your family and with yourself to stay well balanced. Your identity should be much more than being president of a college.

Prioritizing your time is a good technique for achieving balance. Developing a goal of having two meals each day with your family, exercising four times a week, and reading for personal growth two or three hours weekly is recommended. Developing a habit of dating your spouse at least once a week and spending quiet time with your favorite avocation is also a very healthy thing to do. It is important that you try to drop the presidential identity on a regular basis.

Conclusion

As best they can, strong leaders learn to deal with those things that most tempt them in their jobs. Protecting one's status, the desire to be popular, and the need to always maintain harmony among constituents are good examples of temptations that often conflict with good leadership (Lencioni, 1998). Astute leaders examine their weaknesses, accept criticism, and strive to achieve the self-discipline to lead fairly, but effectively. They follow their instincts in making decisions that affect the image, quality, and integrity of the college. They learn how to anticipate reactions from various constituent groups. And they learn how to negotiate so that both parties win. In the end, inspired college leadership is about achieving desired results in a humble and collegial fashion; all the rest is window dressing. These final thoughts are more easily assimilated in their simplest form:

- Make friends
- Never make an enemy

- Be yourself
- Maintain integrity
- Be confident
- Be humble
- Be optimistic
- Have fun

References

Austin, J. (1999). The invisible side of leadership. In F. Hesselbein & P. M. Cohen (Eds.), *Leader to leader: Enduring insights on leadership from the Drucker Foundation's award winning journal* (pp. 375–388). San Francisco: Jossey-Bass.

Desjardins, C., & Huff, S. (2001). *The leading edge: Competencies for community college leadership in the new millennium.* Mission Viejo, CA: National Institute for Leadership Development and League for Innovation in the Community College.

Drucker, P. (1999). My mentor's leadership lessons. In F. Hesselbein & P. M. Cohen (Eds.), *Leader to leader: Enduring insights on leadership from the Drucker Foundation's award winning journal* (pp. 3–7). San Francisco: Jossey-Bass.

Hill, B., Green, M., & Eckel, P. (2001). *What governing boards need to know and do about institutional change.* Washington, DC: American Council on Education.

Knight Higher Education Collaborative. (2001, March). *Policy perspectives.* Philadelphia: Institute for Research on Higher Education.

Lencioni, P. (1998). *The five temptations of a CEO.* San Francisco: Jossey-Bass.

Murphy, E. F. (1978). *Crown treasury of relevant quotations.* New York: Crown Publishers.

Pritchett, P., & Pound, R. (2001). *The stress of organizational change.* Plano, TX: Pritchett Rummler-Brache.

Stuart, L. (1999). *21st century skills for 21st century jobs* (Report). Washington, DC: U.S. Department of Commerce, U.S. Department of Education, U.S. Department of Labor, National Institute for Literacy, and the Small Business Administration.

Vaughn, G. B. 1986. *The community college presidency.* New York: American Council on Education.

About the Authors

GUNDER MYRAN

Gunder Myran is president emeritus of Washtenaw Community College and president of Myran and Associates, a consulting firm focusing on community college and public school leadership. He presently has a long-term consulting relationship with the Wayne County Community College District in Detroit.

Myran served as president of Washtenaw Community College for 23 years (1975–1998). He previously served as an associate professor at Michigan State University (MSU) and held administrative positions at Rockland Community College (New York) and Jackson Community College (Michigan). At MSU, where he earned his doctoral degree, he and Dr. Max Raines led the Kellogg Community College Leadership Program.

Myran has published a number of books and articles on community college leadership, institutional strategy, and continuing education and training. He has served on the board of directors of the American Association of Community Colleges and as board chair for the National Council for Continuing Education and Training (NCCET) and for the Michigan Community College. He received the Thomas J. Peters National Leadership Award from the community college leadership program at the University of Texas and the National Lifetime Achievement Award from the NCCET.

GEORGE A. BAKER III

George A. Baker III was named to the Joseph D. Moore Endowed Chair in Community College Leadership at North Carolina State University (NC State) in 1992 and remained in that position until he retired in 2001. He is the Joseph D. Moore Distinguished University Professor Emeritus at NC State and director of College Planning Systems, a private consulting organization.

Baker has held academic positions including professor of higher and community college education at the University of Texas at Austin, visiting professor at several universities, dean of instruction and vice president for general education at Greenville Technical College, dean of academics at the Marine Corps Educational Center, and professor of management and department head at the Naval War College.

Baker served as first chair of the board of visitors for the Marine Corps University and currently is as board member. He also has served on the board of directors for the American Association of Community Colleges and on the alumni board for Warren Wilson College.

He directed the National Initiative for Leadership and Institutional Effectiveness for nine years and has served as the executive director of the National Alliance of Community and Technical Colleges and of COMBASE.

Baker is a graduate of Warren Wilson [Community] College and of Presbyterian College, where he earned a bachelor's degree in business. He holds a master's degree in counseling psychology (Shippensburg State University) and a master's equivalent degree in public administration (Naval War College). He earned a doctoral degree in education administration from Duke University in 1972.

Since 1970, Baker has provided keynote speeches, consulting, training, and research for more than 750 schools and organizations. He has played a major role in eight national research or development projects involving more than $4 million. His publication credits include more than 250 books, articles, and reports.

Baker has received awards for his research, teaching, service, and national leadership in the community college movement, including, most recently, awards from the governors of Kentucky, Mississippi, and Texas for his contributions to education; the Paul A. Elsner Excellence in Leadership Award; the Jessie Stuart Leadership Recognition Award from the Kentucky Teaching Learning Conference; and a Distinguished Alumnus Award from Warren Wilson College. Early in his career, Baker was awarded the United States Presidential Service Award for his service on Lyndon B. Johnson's military staff and, upon retirement, was awarded the prestigious Order of the Long Leaf Pine from the governor of North Carolina.

BEVERLY SIMONE

Beverly Simone is president of Madison Area Technical College (MATC), a position she has held since 1989. She oversees a student body of more than 50,000, a staff of 3,334, and a total budget of $136 million. She is one of the few women in the nation who heads a public two-year multi-campus college reporting directly to a governing board.

Simone's background includes 33 years as a teacher and administrator in community, vocational, and technical colleges. Prior to assuming her position at MATC, Simone served for two years as the president of Western Wisconsin Technical College in La Crosse, Wisconsin, and in several key administrative positions at MATC from 1980 to 1987. She began her career in technical education at Indiana Vocational Technical College, at which she held a series of increasingly responsible positions during her 10 years at that institution. She holds a BA in speech, theater, and English from Butler University, and an MS in education and communications and an EdD in adult education and higher education administration from Indiana University.

Simone has and continues to serve in national and state leadership roles. She is a member of the national board of directors for American Family Insurance and is a past board chair for the American Association of Community Colleges, the American Association of Women in Community Colleges, and the National Institute for Leadership Development. She has been a board member of the American Council on Education and a trustee on the board of the Higher Learning Commission of the North Central Association of Colleges and Schools.

Simone has been president of the Wisconsin Presidents Association and was selected by her peers to lead the creation and implementation of the eTech College for Wisconsin. She has been named President of the Year by the American Association of Women in Community Colleges and the National Institute for Leadership Development. For her leadership of MATC, she has been recognized by the Consortium for Community College Development as the Best of the Best in organizational transformation and by the NAACP, EEOC, and the League for Innovation. She has also been recognized by the International Women's Forum as a Woman Who Makes A Difference.

TONY ZEISS

Tony Zeiss holds a doctorate in community college administration, a master's degree in speech (radio and television), and a bachelor's degree in speech education. In 1992, Zeiss became the third president of Central Piedmont Community College (CPCC), the largest college in North Carolina serving approximately 70,000 students per year. During his tenure, the college has grown from one campus to six and has become recognized as a national leader in workforce development. Zeiss has authored or co-authored several books on economic development, adult literacy, and national workforce development. His most recent publications include three books on creating high performance employees, a novel based on the Civil War, and a book on community college leadership. Zeiss has published more than 50 professional articles, papers, and research documents and more than 400 newspaper columns.

Zeiss is a professional speaker and a member of the National Speaker's Association. He is a frequent keynoter for companies and colleges on recruiting, developing, and retaining peak performers in the workplace. He regularly consults with states and regions on economic development.

Zeiss is past chair of the board of the American Association of Community Colleges and was a member of the U.S. Vice President's 21st Century Workforce Development Leadership Task Force in 1999–2000. In 1998, he represented America's community colleges at the UNESCO World Conference on Higher Education in Paris. Zeiss is the North Carolina Community College System's President of the Year for 2002, and CPCC was selected as the 2002 Community College of the Year by the National Alliance of Business.

Zeiss serves on several local, regional, and national boards and is a member of the National Commission on NAEP (National Assessment Governing Board) 12th Grade Assessment Reporting and is a member of the advisory panel for the U. S. Department of Education Office of Vocational and Adult Education.

Index